A Guid

to

‘The Learning Adventure’

by

Eva Hoffman

Illustrations by Justina Langley

First published in Great Britain in 1999

Cover design and illustrations by Justina Langley

ISBN 0 9535387 1 0

Published by:
LEARN TO LEARN
PO Box 29,
Middlewich,
CW10 9FN, UK
Tel +44 (0)1606 832 895
Fax +44 (0)1606 837 645

Printed in England

A Guide

to

'The Learning Adventure'

Eva Hoffman

a note from the publisher

The success of 'The Learning Adventure' and the overwhelmingly positive reactions we have received have made us realize that the need for help and advice in this crucial area of our lives is even greater than we thought.
This guide book is a response to many requests from parents and teachers wanting to 'know more' and seeking reassurance that they were making the best possible use of 'The Learning Adventure' workbook.
We enclose here a few extracts from comments made by some of the more prominent readers/users of 'The Learning Adventure', all of them seasoned practitioners - our hope is that, if needed, it may give some of you an extra dose of reassurance and encouragement to ***try it out*** *and* confidence that it is all worthwhile.

> *" 'The Learning Adventure' is a treasure trove of ideas... I love it. Every child should have the chance to do the 'Learn to Learn' course. And what a difference it would make to our schools if every teacher did it!"*
> - Susan Norman, author and publisher, NLP practitioner

> *" 'The Learning Adventure' is a pure feast for famished juveniles - no school should be without it...*
> *all the new ideas rigorously presented behind a nourishing text of such delicacy and charm that it could not fail to melt the most sceptical teenagers...*
> *This is a book with a potential to transform thousands of lives."*
> - Grethe Hooper Hansen, international suggestopedia consultant, former director of SEAL - Society for Effective Affective Learning

> *" What a fabulous contribution to the world! The book is both useful and inspiring, offering a vision of learning as a real adventure... and covers key elements vital to easy and natural learning for children of all ages."*
> - David Orr, TOC, International Buzan Centres instructor

> *" 'The Learning Adventure' is a beautiful, friendly, and fun guide to learning... encouraging children to open up to themselves, to the world, and providing them with*

a tool kit for adventure of life-long learning."
- Titus Alexander, Chair, Westminster UNA Charter for Global Governance

" 'The Learning Adventure' is a truly beautiful book; ... Children that are given a copy will indeed be lucky; they can't fail to benefit from the ideas and the splendid way they are presented. It will be a wonderful investment for their futures."
- Murray White, educational consultant, British Representative for the International Council for Self Esteem

"A child I know, who is bright, but would be (let me be honest, is!) not very easy to have in a class, picked the book up, flicked over the pages, and settled on one that seemed to interest him. After a while he took the book up to his room. In the end he spent the whole weekend working through it - engaged, delighted, sharing it with friends...
It is part of the quality of this book that it reaches children at a serious and affirmative level. There are hints for accepting criticism, brain gym exercises, mind mapping exercises and a host of learning tools, any one of which would transform a routine lesson into a star rated event."
- Rev David Barton

"At last! A book about HOW to learn instead of WHAT to learn. But there are hundreds of them already, you may be thinking. Not like this one! Not written for children in simple clear language, without ever being patronising...
The enthusiastic reaction that the book received is easy to understand, as for any sensitive teacher or parent it embraces the very essence of growing and learning...
Eva Hoffman's book could create a generation of sensitive adults which would make the third millennium one to look forward to...
What a very different world this would be if everybody read and followed 'The Learning Adventure'!
- Izabella Hearn, teacher, author, Director of SEAL Spain (extracts from the book review in SEAL Newsletter, 1999/2)

We hope you find this book not only useful but inspirational, helping you in making your whole learning adventure an even more exciting and fulfilling process.

Contents

Contents

Contents

a word before you start...

a word before you start...

Dear Parent,

Dear Teacher,

Dear Educator,

Have you ever thought why children never give up when they are learning to walk, to talk, to dress themselves, or to climb stairs?

It may well be because:

- children are born with the ability to acquire those skills,
- very small children don't know that it is possible not to learn,
- children practise, practise, and practise, until they succeed (giving up is not on the agenda!),
- children learn by imitating others but do it in their own way and their own time,
- we expect children to learn these skills,
- we give them constant support and encouragement,
- we smile, we praise and applaud every success, no matter how small.

In other words, children have learning ingrained in them. They believe they can do it. They learn by observing us, and then by endless repetitions undertaken in their own way and in their own time. We, in turn, have positive expectations, and give children a lot of encouragement and support, whenever we feel they need it.

Although during the first few years of their lives all healthy children find it exciting to learn new skills and to acquire new information, many of them seem to lose their enthusiasm for learning as they get a little older. At school they have little or no control over what they learn and how they learn it, the two things which mass education cannot possibly do for them.

What is more, children have no conscious understanding of their unique learning styles and no learning tools to assist their specific needs. There are children who manage well without the awareness of their preferred learning styles, and who are lucky enough to stumble across some suitable tools which they successfully use to their advantage. Many, however, never find out how they could learn best. As a result, they often fall behind, failing to meet their teachers' and parents' expectations. Failure to perform well frequently takes away children's confidence and dramatically lowers their self-esteem. They begin living under constant pressure, with high levels of stress dominating their lives.

Most children are survivors and bravely soldier on. Some, however, find it very difficult, regardless of how bright and intelligent they may be. Research shows that stress and low self-esteem are responsible for most learning difficulties. This is why many children fall behind more and more, and for many the downward spiral stops only when they leave school. It breaks any parent's heart to see their child discouraged, disappointed and unhappy.

The very fact that you have bought 'The Learning Adventure' means that you are interested in helping children, your own or others, to learn more effectively.

I would like to share with you a few thoughts I believe to be of paramount importance for the learning adventure programme to work.

All children are born learners.

Everybody who has observed a child grow has seen endless

examples to support the above statement. Children demonstrate it beautifully in the first years of their lives, forever surprising us with their newly acquired skills and knowledge about the world. For all small children learning is a way of life, the most natural and enjoyable activity taking up all their waking time.

It is possible to rekindle the natural joy and enthusiasm for learning.

When you decide to guide your children along the path towards discovering their true potential, their sense of enjoyment, and the awareness that learning is great fun, I suggest you do whatever you can to find your own enthusiasm for learning. If you do this, you will have a greater chance to see this happen in your children, and you may at the same time re-discover the joy of spending quality time with them.

ENTHUSIASM IS CONTAGIOUS!

Every child learns differently.

Every child is absolutely unique and because of that every child learns best in his or her own, unique way. People differ in the ways they receive information and in the ways they process the information in their brains. Carla Hannaford [1)] identifies as many as 32 different basic learning profiles which, combined with other preferences of a learner, constitute his or her individual, unique learning style. Schools, with all the effort they make, cannot cater for the specific needs of every individual child. This is where well-informed parents can step in and do a great deal to help!

One person who believes in the child can make an enormous difference.

All educators, whether they are teachers, parents, mentors, or other caring individuals, have to believe in the possibility of making a significant positive difference in children's lives. Without a strong conviction that children are capable of changing their attitudes, of improving their performance, there is hardly any point embarking on the whole venture. It may not be easy if you are a true sceptic and think that this programme is yet another thing you simply have to try in order to clear your conscience, to know that you have done everything possible to help your child learn. It is vital that you find it in your heart to really, genuinely believe in your child.

It often takes just one person to change dramatically children's attitudes towards themselves, to inspire them, help them believe in themselves and start them on the road to success. There are many, wonderfully inspiring anecdotes, that prove this beyond any reasonable doubt. It may be the child's teacher, parent, or grandparent. It may be YOU.

Learning is an inseparable part of life, and that is why it makes sense to view it in the context of all the aspects of a child's life experience and to look at a child as the whole person rather than as the learning brain. Developing one skill, practising one aspect of the process, is similar to exercising the muscles of one leg and expecting to become a fast runner. Runners, for example, need to exercise all their muscles, practise breathing, develop their stamina and positive mental attitude, in order to improve their results. Similarly, if we want our children to find their unique way of learning well, it is essential that we work simultaneously on all aspects related to the learning process.

'The Learning Adventure' has been divided into five main sections. Separating one aspect of learning from another is very artificial; the natural way would be to organise the material into units, every one composed of one or two activities/exercises, taken from each of the five sections. However, I stayed with the artificial arrangement to let you, and the children you work with, be more flexible in choosing your exercises, and to let you be the judge of the best order in which you wish to proceed.

Before getting acquainted with some of the elements that constitute children's learning experience and seeing what you can do to bring the enthusiasm and joy of learning back into their lives, I would like you to consider a few suggestions based on my experience of working with children.

You are in it, too!

The learning to learn programme has been a big discovery adventure, not only for the children I have worked with, but for me as well! This may come as a surprise to you but when you start preparing the exercises, you will soon know what I mean.

Don't worry if many ideas in the book seem new to you, or even strange. Many groundbreaking discoveries have been made in the last 20 years. A lot of the brilliant and fascinating ideas recently conceived and put into practical use are new also to us, professionals.

In order to go through this programme and be of true help to your child, you may need to open your mind to new ideas. Some exercises may bring up in you protest and resentment, maybe unpleasant memories of long forgotten (?) childhood experiences. I think it would be most valuable if you could share some of your childhood experiences with your child, even those which reveal your weaknesses and disappointments.

Children value honesty and appreciate openness. Find the courage to show your vulnerability and hurt: this will make you more 'human' and closer to the child, easier to relate to. This can dramatically improve your relationship and bring you much closer together. View it as a wonderful 'by-product' and embrace the opportunity!

Your preparation

I suggest that you read the explanations and exercises a day or two in advance. This way you will give yourself time to think about the ideas and about the way of relating them to your child's experience.

Sometimes you may also want to mention some ideas in passing and leave them with the children for a day or two, letting them 'brew' for a while (the ideas, not the children!)

Many of the exercises, particularly from 'Smile at Yourself', may have a powerful effect on children; it is important that you make every possible effort to end the day on a positive note, having dispersed the child's doubts, sadness, insecurities, and negative thoughts.

Timing and the mood

Choose the right moment to work with your children. All of you should be in a good mood, well rested, willing to be together, feeling you have all the time in the world to yourselves, even if it happens to be only half an hour.

It will all make much more sense when your children WANT to participate in the adventure and when you can make it a happy event for all concerned. The adventure time is meant to be enjoyable and bring in the sense of fun and joy.

Parents are often busy, worried, tired, and irritable. When planning to work with your child, do whatever you can to create in yourself a peaceful and serene mood: play some relaxing music, read a page from an inspiring book, meditate, or dance. Do whatever works for you. Only when you are ready, invite your child to join you in the learning fun.

When I work with children, I make a point of remembering some 'ins and outs' which make work more enjoyable and effective:

In:	Out:
gentle encouragement	forcing
invitation	pushing /pressure
relaxed mood	tense atmosphere
pleasantness	irritation
praise	criticism
'all the time in the world'	hurry
choice	compulsion

With or without a friend?

If there is just one particular child you want to work with, try encouraging her or him to invite a friend whose company they enjoy; if they don't want anybody to join in the activities, accept their decision.

Smaller children may be happy to do exercises in the company of their pets or cuddly toys.

Suggestions for planning your sessions

Week-end sessions:

During the Saturday and Sunday five-hour sessions, try the following:

- a deep relaxation (see the companion CD, track 1),
- a Helicopter Spin,
- a Cross-Pat and a Cross-Walk;
- 5 self-esteem, 2 relaxation, 2 concentration, 3-4 discovering how you learn and 2-3 learning tools exercises.

Children will need to take breaks, probably every 35-45 minutes, depending on the type of activity they engage in.

Every 15-20 minutes do a 'mini' relaxation exercise, such as Cat Stretch, Neck Rub, Shoulder Massage, or Yawn, and remind everybody about deep breathing.

Encourage children to drink water (bottled still or tap) and move around during the breaks.

Regular weekly sessions:

During the two-hour sessions, consider doing:

deep relaxation, a Helicopter Spin and a Cross-Walk, and one exercise from each of the five parts of the book.

The number and the times of breaks will depend on the day, on how children feel, and on the type of activities you engage in.

Again, remind the children to drink water during their breaks.

Random sessions:

Only the deep relaxation, the Helicopter Spin and the Cross-Pat/ Walk/Doodle exercises are the fixed parts of the routine.

If you decide to do self-esteem exercises, select 2 or 3 and let the child choose one of them. Do that with every part of the book.

How much you do will depend on the time available and, most importantly, on how the children respond.

Photographs

Take three smiling pictures of the children: one on their own, others with their favourite people, pets, toys, or other objects. It's good to have the pictures developed before you start working through the 'adventure' exercises. They will be useful for self-esteem and relaxation exercises.

Books / materials

Ideally, every child ought to have his/her own, very private and very personal copy of the workbook.

Ask the children what colours they like best and, if possible, let them write and draw on sheets in their preferred colours.

Equipment

Here is a list of things you may find useful:

- a word-processor or a type-writer
- a CD player
- comfortable mats to lie on
- big cushions to sit on
- lap-top trays/desks
- ring-binders
- coloured paper,
- coloured markers (thick and thin)
- crayons, pens, pencils

- finger paints
- thick, red felt
- candles
- a big clock

and anything you can think of to make it fun!

The place

Make the room where you spend the 'adventure time' with the children bright and cosy.

There are children who don't particularly care about those things, but for many, working in a nice, pleasant environment makes a big difference.

Make an effort to decorate the room in such a way that it is a joy for all of you to spend time in it.

smile at yourself

smile at yourself

Healthy self-esteem: liking yourself and believing in yourself.

During the first few years of their lives most children believe they can do it all. To protect them from disappointment and from getting hurt, both physically and emotionally, we start making them aware of all kinds of problems, difficulties and obstacles, and slowly but firmly make them realise that in fact they cannot do it all. Then it somehow goes a little too far and, before we know it, we start hearing statements like: 'I can't do it', 'I can never do it!', 'I am not good at it', 'I cannot do anything right!', 'you do it for me'. Many children soon learn to give up trying and to stop making an effort.

Why does it happen?

There may be quite a few reasons, but probably the most important one is that they no longer believe they are capable of achieving whatever they want to achieve, so why bother trying?

The importance of good self-esteem and self-confidence cannot be over-emphasised. Good self-image, healthy self-esteem and well-grounded self-confidence are some of the essential ingredients of success in learning and happiness in life.

Working on your child's self-esteem may prove to be a real challenge because, as Murray White [2)] rightly observes, self-esteem cannot be taught. Luckily, it can be learned. “If we wish to raise a child's self-esteem, our job is to create an environment, and provide experience, which will help the child discover how to learn it for himself”.

Nathaniel Branden [3)] sees the following factors as essential for nurturing a child's self-esteem:

Basic Safety and Security

A safe and secure environment is needed to bring up a person who can later learn to trust themselves, a person with a confident sense of boundaries.

Touch

Touch is the most powerful way in which we convey love, caring, comfort, support, and nurturing. It is essential for a child's healthy development.

Love

A child treated with love learns to see himself as loveable. An angry parent must learn not to withdraw love. Love for your children must be unconditional, but it does not mean there is nothing for them to learn. It means: ' You have value, you are precious the way you are; you don't need to do anything or be like anybody to be loved!' The attitude 'I will love you when you do X, if you behave Y, if you perform Z', does not make the child feel loved.

Acceptance

Acceptance is shown by listening to and acknowledging the child's thoughts and feelings (not by arguing, lecturing, 'psychologizing' or insulting!). It is extremely helpful if the child's nature, temperament, interests, and aspirations are accepted, whether the parents share them or not. Self-esteem will grow if differences are accepted.

Respect

A child who is treated with respect tends to learn self-respect and tends to treat others with respect and courtesy. Courtesy when addressing the child and treating the child as a person in his/her own rights is indispensable, if we want to bring up a person with a healthy self-esteem.

Psychological Visibility

We all need to receive from other human beings an appropriate feedback. We are superficially visible to most people but we need a few, or at least one, who will make us feel truly visible. Psychological visibility means: 'I feel seen, heard, and understood by you'. Psychological invisibility brings pain, insecurity and low self-esteem. "When we convey love, appreciation, empathy, acceptance, respect, we make a child visible". (Branden[3)], p. 182)

Age - appropriate Nurturing

Different forms of nurturing are right for different ages. A parent's goal is to support the child's independence. The child needs to be encouraged to make choices appropriate to the level of his or her stage of development. When people are adults and they are still emotionally immature, their self-esteem suffers.

Praise and Criticism

It is important to distinguish between evaluative praise and appreciative praise. Judgmental, evaluative praise, such as: 'good girl', 'you're doing great', invites dependency on other people's judgement. To be one's own person, a child must be free from the pressure of evaluative praise.

Appreciative praise describes the child's behaviour. Instead of saying; *Good boy, you have tidied your mess at last*, say: *All your books are on the shelves, the toys are arranged neatly in boxes, and there is so much space on the floor! It must have been a lot of work but you did it!*

After you have described what you see, children will evaluate their behaviour for themselves.

It is important to criticise the behaviour, not the child.

Say what you see, how you feel, and say what you want the child to do, but don't put the child down: *You have hurt your little brother's arm and he is crying because it hurts him a lot. I am very angry and I want you to apologise to him. No? Well, then go to your room and think about what you ought to do!* Omit: *You horrible little rascal, you never think how others feel, do you?!*

NO ONE WAS EVER MADE GOOD
BY BEING INFORMED HE OR SHE WAS BAD!

Parental Expectations

Children feel secure when they know what is expected of them. Rational parents let the children know what ethical standards and what performance they expect of their children.

Dealing with Mistakes

The way parents respond to mistakes greatly influences children's self-esteem. We all make mistakes. Mistakes are a part of learning and making progress. Fear of making mistakes paralyses creativity, stops children from trying out new things, and puts them under tremendous pressure. There is a big difference between striving to perform better, to achieve better results, and being a perfectionist. A child who is put down for making a mistake will quickly learn to put him/herself down.

There are more factors which need to be looked at when we want to enhance self-esteem in children. Let us consider two of them:

Promises: Keeping vs. Breaking

Every time we break a promise made to others, or to ourselves, our self-esteem goes down. When we keep promises, particularly when it is not very easy to do what we have promised and decided to do, our self-esteem soars to the sky. Goals are promises too. Children who learn to set goals for themselves and to achieve them have a good chance to succeed in many ways and to enjoy healthy self-esteem.

Competition: Winning and Losing

Many people believe that competition is a part of life and that winning in competition secures good self-esteem. Others seriously doubt the benefits of competition, particularly in the area of education, and see it as a potential danger.

In competition there is usually only one winner and many more losers; no matter how good you are, you may still lose and, if you are not careful, you may lose your self-esteem in the process.

Competing means attempting to prove that you can do something better than others. How about showing children that the best and most valid competition is competition with themselves?

Try saying: 'Be better than you were last time, last month, in your last exam'. This way the child hardly ever loses and her or his self-esteem improves rather than diminishes.

I often wonder whether there is anything more difficult than being a parent. Probably not. Then again, not many other experiences will teach you as many lessons and simply force you to grow and develop the way parenting does. That has certainly been true for me.

The exercises in **smile at yourself** suggest what you can do to help our children learn how to accept themselves and to enhance their own self-esteem. This will boost their self-confidence so that you may once again hear them say:

I LIKE MYSELF

I KNOW I AM SPECIAL AND UNIQUE

I KNOW I CAN LEARN ANYTHING I WANT!

I BELIEVE I CAN DO IT!

Exercises

LIKING YOURSELF AND BELIEVING IN YOURSELF

Read the text before you give it to your children and think which of the following suggestions would be most appropriate for them:

- you could ask them to read the text for themselves and to tell you what they think it is about
- you could read the text to them and ask them questions, such as:

    Who are the people who believe in you?

    Do you like yourself?

    What is it that you like about yourself?

    Do you have friends who believe in their ability to succeed?

    Do you know people who clearly do not have confidence in themselves?

    What difference does it make whether people believe in themselves or not?

Give examples of people you know and how their self-esteem influences their lives.

Have a rubber ball and a blob of plasticine or BLU-TACK ready. Let the child play with it and demonstrate how important it is to have a self-esteem that bounces back whenever, and for whatever reason, it goes down.

YOUR INNER WEATHER REPORT

Taking time to look 'into' yourself and becoming aware of the way you feel is a good way to start your day. It's wonderful if you realise you feel happy and ready to face the day; it is necessary to be aware of any feelings of sadness, unhappiness, or nervousness, so that you can try to do something about them.

Read the text aloud slowly, using your gentle sounding voice and remembering to breathe every time you pause.

Let the child draw the picture first, then talk about it a little: you can ask the child to explain the picture to you. Be gentle and ask few questions, particularly if the picture is rainy or stormy. If the weather is 'bad', do the visualisation exercise ('More about your inner weather').

Before you start reading, make sure the child is sitting or lying comfortably; dim the lights and close the door, asking people present in the house to respect your 'private time'.

Put on some relaxing music (see the companion CD) and ask the child whether he or she is happy with the music or whether they prefer complete silence.

Read slowly, using your soft, gentle voice. While reading, imagine that you are doing this exercise yourself. It will help you read at the right pace. Pause for long, relaxed breaths. When you get to the end ("...the sun in your heart"), make a long pause.

It is extremely important to get out of the deeply relaxed state very slowly. With some children this 'coming back' process may take a long time. Just watch your child carefully and you will *feel* when the time is right.

If the second drawing is not a happier one, it may be necessary to encourage the children to talk about their feelings. Be gentle and tactful; pushing too hard causes resentment and anger. If they are upset, you may tell them that you are always ready to listen, whenever they want to talk. It is, however, advisable to end the session on a positive note, so make every effort to uplift the child's mood.

HAPPY WORDS AND NASTY WORDS

The language we use has much more significance than many of us realise. Help children become aware of the language they use and develop their sensitivity to it. The words we use program our brain in the way specialists program computers. The difference is that it is easier to delete a computer program than to get rid of a negative 'program' in the brain.

Show your children how the language they use influences the way they feel. You may ask them to write down two groups of sentences, such as:

> *It's horrible. I hate this kind of weather. I feel rotten. Nobody understands me.*
>
> *How lovely. What beautiful flowers. I want to jump for joy. You are a great friend.*

These are only examples. It's best if you think of sentences relevant to your child's life. It will be even better if you let the children think of their own 'good' and 'nasty' things to say. Ask the children to tell you how it makes them feel when they hear or say those things. The more nasty and negative things we say, the worse we feel. Try it with your children and experience the downward spiral of your mood. It is perfectly possible to make yourself feel absolutely awful in a matter of minutes! Unless you enjoy this state of mind, let's look at the ways to stop this destructive overflow.

The thing to do is not necessarily to withdraw the negative language from your vocabulary altogether. A few minutes of moaning is something we occasionally enjoy, maybe even need...

It is, however, vital to know when enough is enough, when to stop moaning and groaning, complaining, cursing the world, and criticising everything and everybody.

Don't expect that a few exercises can rid your children (or you, for that matter) of a life-long habit, but they will make the children more sensitive to the effect their language has on their lives.

Erasing destructive language along with destructive thoughts is the first step. Imagine a whiteboard with all the negative words and phrases you tend to use. Take a board wiper and swiftly wipe the board clean.

The second step is filling your mind (which does not tolerate a vacuum) with the thoughts you want. Imagine writing them in beautiful colours on the whiteboard.

Do it again and again: wipe the thoughts/words you don't want off the board and replace them with the ones you do want.

IT IS NECESSARY TO BE ABLE TO DO IT YOURSELF BEFORE YOU START HELPING OTHER PEOPLE.

Helping others is often very challenging. We try saying something positive, but it may well be the very last thing the person wants to hear! Helping others in an effective way requires great sensitivity: sensitivity to people's feelings and a sensitive use of language.

This exercise will not only make the children more sensitive to other people's feelings and needs but will also show them how they can help others as well as themselves.

Talk with the children about things that help you, and encourage them to tell you what it is that they find helpful.

THE MAGIC BOX

Find two boxes: one for your child and the other for yourself, and have fun making them beautiful. Let both of you look around the house for some wonderfully uplifting things, such as postcards from friends, photographs, pictures, pebbles, shells, letters from people who love you, just anything that will make you feel good and smile. A box like that is truly magical on days when things don't go exactly the way we would like them to (and what a wonderful understatement it is, too!). Try it, and see for yourself.

YOU ARE ABSOLUTELY UNIQUE

It is a fact proved to be true beyond any reasonable doubt that no two people in this world are exactly the same. We are all unique, and this makes us all special.

Play an association game with your children. Here is one way you can play it:

Give the children any word you think of, and ask them to write any other word that comes to mind in connection with this word. And again, what comes to mind in connection with the second word, and so on. Ask the children to write chains of ten words, each word associated with the previous one.

For example:

an apple - apple-tree - garden - orchard - picnic - basket - sandwiches - bread - butter - milk - cow;

or:

an apple - apple-pie - baking - flour - dough - kitchen - oven - hot - burn - smoke - fire - fire-brigade, etc.

It is, of course, possible, that some words will appear on other people's lists; nevertheless, every child's association chain will be different.

A game like this shows the uniqueness of our minds, and proves that we are all special and different.

Ideally, three or more people should do this exercise. The more people do it, the better it will document our uniqueness. It will also be more fun!

YOUR WONDERFUL CHARACTERISTICS

The older children get, the more challenging it is for them to speak well about themselves. It becomes somehow easier for them to put themselves down than to say good things about characteristics of their personalities.

In order to enhance children's self-esteem we need to help them reverse this tendency, which is deeply rooted in our culture and reinforced by our upbringing.

Do these exercises yourself before giving them to your child. Become aware of the feelings they bring up in you. You may be quite happy to fill the blanks, but it is possible that you will find it challenging. The same may be true for your child. Should this be the case, gently prompt the possible answers. If, however, this proves to be an unpleasant experience, leave the exercises incomplete, saying you may be coming back to them later.

It is vital that at some point they are tackled again. Try as many times as it takes, until children feel comfortable doing them.

GOOD WORDS FOR YOUR MAGIC BOX

When planning to do this exercise, alert your family members and close friends that they may be asked by the children to write short notes saying why they like or love them and what they appreciate about them. This is one of the most powerful exercises in the book. I suggest you copy 'your smiling picture' drawing onto a larger (A3 ?) sheet of paper and that you are the first person to write your note in one of the frames. Ideally, your child could ask other members of your family members and family friends to fill the remaining frames.

Prompt the child to say: 'Please write in this frame why you like me and what you appreciate about me'. If saying it makes the child uncomfortable, the request for a note could be given in writing. If this proves too difficult as well, you may need to step in and do the asking on the child's behalf.

When all the frames have been filled, have the child read the comments aloud and then hang the sheet up on the wall in his or her room where it can be easily seen. After a while the sheet can find its way to the Magic Box to be kept and cherished.

It is often a truly moving experience to see in black and white how others feel about us and why they appreciate us!

GOOD THINGS IN YOUR LIFE

The importance of appreciating who we are and what we have cannot be overemphasised.

Truly appreciative people are generally content with their lives and hardly ever get depressed or miserable. If they do, the negative feelings last only for a short while.

Making a list of things we appreciate in our lives seems an easy enough task to complete, and yet it is not always so, particularly when we are asked to do it for the first time, and when we have never ever thought about it.

Here is what you can prompt to get your children started:

I have enough food whenever I need it.

I can see and I can hear.

There are people who love me very much.

My Mum is always there for me.

My bed is cosy and warm.

My Granny takes me on holidays.

My pet is always happy to see me.

I go to visit interesting places.

Get your child (and yourself!) into a habit of taking time every evening to make a list of all the good things that happened to her or him that day.

I had Wheetos for breakfast. I love Wheetos!

My good friend came to see me.

I got a card from my grandmother.

My brother shared his crisps with me.

We visited beautiful water gardens in Cheshire.

There is no need to wait until somebody gives you a Ferrari or invites you for a holiday in the Bahamas to appreciate life.

LEARN TO ENJOY LITTLE THINGS.
IT WILL MAKE YOU A MUCH HAPPIER PERSON!

BE YOUR OWN BEST FRIEND

Many of us tend to talk negatively about ourselves and criticise the things we do only too frequently. This has somehow become an 'in-thing' to do.

How stupid of me!

I can never get it right!

My memory is going. What was I thinking about?!

I could never ever learn to use a computer!

My hair looks so ugly!

At the same time we think other people are luckier, cleverer, stronger, more creative, more able; they have more friends, wear more attractive clothes, and are better at games. The interesting thing is that very often those very people think similar things about us!

The healthiest thing your child can do is to stop comparing him/ herself with others.

Have you ever written a full characteristic of your children? I am sure that many times you talked about their talents and their merits, as well as about their negative characteristics and difficulties. However, I do suggest that this time you put it in writing. Observe your children carefully for a few days in a detached manner, as if you were a complete stranger. If your experience is similar to mine, your will find it a fascinating adventure, very revealing, and full of surprises. There is a strong possibility you will make some wonderful discoveries and feel that the exercise has helped you know your child better!

Tell your son how special he is; show your daughter how unique she is. Discuss with them their various characteristics, their strengths and weaknesses, their special qualities and gifts.

Tell them time and time again to like themselves and to accept who they are. Tell them they can improve, get better at whatever they choose to do.

But liking themselves and self-acceptance must come first.

LABELS, LABELS, LABELS...

Tell your child about a label somebody stuck on you when you were still at school. Tell them about the hurt and anger, and maybe some lasting consequences. If you were lucky not to be labelled in your childhood, tell them about somebody you knew who suffered because of negative labelling.

Ask you children whether somebody has stuck labels on them and to tell you what it felt like. Does it still hurt when they think about it?

Ask the children whether they have been putting labels on others and have them imagine how those people must have felt.

Retaliation is the most common form of defence: one person hurts another, so they hurt in return*: I am not stupid! You are an idiot!*

And so it goes: hurt, more hurt, and a violent outburst.

Tell the children that the fact that they have done something stupid doesn't make them stupid; the fact that they have told lies doesn't make them liars. Sometimes they do silly things, sometimes they behave in a perfectly reasonable way; sometimes they tell lies and on other occasions they are truthful and honest. The same is true about everybody else!

The essence of dealing with harmful labelling is to learn to differentiate between the *person* and *their behaviour*.

Ask your child if they remember the last time they acted with love and respect, and when they behaved in a horribly cruel way; when they were truthful and caring, and when they lied and said nasty words to others. Good understanding of the difference between one and the other is essential for all the exercises dealing with labels. Once the difference between: *I hate you* and *I hate what you've done* is really understood and felt, we are nearly there!

PROTECT YOUR FEELING OF SELF-WORTH

Nobody can give us good self-esteem, no matter how hard they try. Nobody can teach us to have it, either. We have to learn it and accept that we are fully responsible for the way we feel about ourselves. When our self-esteem is in poor shape, the praise others shower us with might make us feel a little better but only for a while. The good feeling will soon vanish, and we will find ourselves waiting for more praise, expecting others to do it again.

Help your children become independent of praise coming from others. People don't always praise us; indeed there are times when we feel that nobody has anything good to say about who we are and what we do. Your children need to build solid foundations for their self-esteem so that it is strong and reliable in times when things don't go too well.

YOUR PICTURE OF YOURSELF

If you see yourself as a successful, competent, able person - this is who you are.
If you see yourself as a failure, as an incompetent and stupid person - this is who you are.

The way we see ourselves is essential for the way we experience life. All of us have successes and failures, do sensible and silly things, act competently and make a mess of things. The important thing is what it is you focus on: your failures or your successes.

Read the text, give it some thought, and, as usual, do the exercises yourself before giving them to your child. Ask your children to look in the mirror and to tell you what the person they see in the mirror is like, what they look like, and how they feel about themselves.

Children often start fooling around to cover their embarrassment, not knowing what to say. Go along with the silliness; as you may have noticed it yourself, it is quite a challenge to answer those seemingly simple questions!

Many children may be a little puzzled and not know what to say. You can help by asking questions. Alternatively, you may suggest that the person they see may appear to them to be kind, loving, clever, pretty, gifted, and friendly. It is, however, possible that they insist on seeing someone who appears to be too fat/thin, ugly, stupid, clumsy, and truly nasty. If you child sees him or herself as possessing many negative characteristics, try one of the following suggestions:

Look at the child and tell them what person YOU see. For example say:

' I can see a charming girl who is sensitive, who cares about her family and friends, who is kind to animals, who is determined to be good at riding/science, and who at the moment appears to be upset and fails to appreciate her good qualities'.

'I can see a boy who is loving and caring, who has a great sense of humour, and a lot of courage and determination. He sometimes expects perfection from himself and seems to forget that everybody makes mistakes and that it may take some time to succeed'.

Find all the good characteristics in your child and talk about them in a matter-of-fact manner, avoiding exaggeration and strongly emotional words such as 'wonderful', 'brilliant' or 'fantastic'. They serve little purpose and, if anything, have an opposite effect from the one you intend.

Some of the exercises in this section, e.g. 'You are absolutely unique' or 'Be your own best friend', may have to be repeated time and time again, if you discover that your child's self-image needs to be modified.

Talk about the importance of good self-image, and be prepared that it may take quite some time before you achieve your goal.

MY TEACHER, MR. MISTAKE

Can you remember some dreadful mistake you have made and

the terrible embarrassment that accompanied it? Most of us have made mistakes that make us blush every time we think about them.

The fear of making mistakes can be paralysing, and the ancient saying: *'making mistakes is human'* seems to be of little help. Making mistakes makes us lose face, makes us appear stupid and inadequate. Since we tend to think we should be perfect in everything we do and of course be always right, being wrong is often the worst thing that can happen to us.

And yet, we all make mistakes!

And we don't always have to be right!

Talk to your children about your mistakes, as well as about some important or silly mistakes their grandfather, uncle, friends and other people they know have made. The only bad thing about making mistakes is not learning anything from them. What is more, most of us need to make the same mistake over and over again before we really learn!

Do whatever you can to ensure that your child accepts mistakes as an inseparable part of learning. Teach them to admit they have made a mistake and, if possible, correct it. We not only learn more that way: life becomes much easier if we can do it!

BELIEVE IN YOURSELF

Saying loud and with conviction:

I BELIEVE IN ME

I BELIEVE I CAN LEARN WHATEVER I WANT

has for many children been a turning point in their experience with learning.

As I have already said, very young children take success for granted and are delighted with everything they do. However, as they grow older, this positive self-image often seems to vanish, to be replaced by a lot of negativity and self-doubt.

To start believing in themselves again, every child needs at least one person to genuinely believe in them. Let it be YOU.

PROMISES, PROMISES

We make many promises every day: *I'll call you, I'll send it to you tomorrow, I'll answer letters the day I receive them, I'll lose a stone by Christmas.*

Children make different promises: *I'll be nice to my brother, I'll do my homework before I go to play, I'll remember to brush my teeth every night.*

Making and keeping promises, in other words setting goals for yourself and achieving them, is vital for a successful life. A promise kept, a goal achieved, boosts your self-esteem; a promise broken does the exact opposite. It weakens your self-respect and makes your self-esteem go down.

Start practising with your child the art of goal setting. Do it together: let the child know what goal you are setting for yourself and let him or her tell you what their goal is. Ensure that the goal is positive, obtainable, and short-term. When both of you have achieved your goals, celebrate your success and make it known to other members of the family.

Teach your children to write down their goals. When you write it, it somehow becomes more real, more serious. It is advisable for writing down goals to become a habit. Encourage your children to write down their weekly goals, and record their progress. The goal's wording needs to be positive, e.g.:

I will grow my finger-nails,

rather than:

I won't bite my finger-nails;

I will keep my room tidy,

rather than:

I won't make a mess.

Every achieved goal, no matter how small, is a boost to a person's self-esteem.

THE ART OF WISE SELF-CONFIDENCE

When we are angry or upset, when we disagree with somebody, when someone has been unfair, has hurt our feelings or has done something wrong, we can behave in three different ways.

Option a): We may choose to shout, scream, or become verbally or physically aggressive. This behaviour is often confused with self-confidence and good self-esteem; in fact, it indicates that the person is not in control of their emotions and lacks interpersonal skills. This option is never beneficial because while it hurts and offends other people, it also hurts us, leaving us with a feeling of inadequacy and a bad aftertaste.

Option b): We may opt for saying nothing, 'bottle up' the feelings of hurt and anger and pretend that nothing has happened. In a number of situations this option is less harmful than the previous one and in the short run may even be beneficial. However, as the only or most frequent response to difficult situations, it is bound to lower our self-esteem dramatically. It may also eventually lead to some kind of explosion, e.g. a sudden outburst of rage accompanied by dangerously violent behaviour, or in some cases a physical illness.

Option c): We may firmly express our thoughts and feelings using acceptable language, and trying not to hurt the other person. Every time we behave this way our respect for ourselves grows. The ability to control our emotions gives us genuine satisfaction. This is the perfection many of us are struggling to achieve, sometimes succeeding, at other times not.

Since all education starts with awareness, making your child aware of the options is the first step on the way to wise self-confidence.

The exercises in this section create a challenge not only for young children but for us, adults, as well. As we grow older (and wiser...) it becomes easier, but for most of us reacting with wise self-confidence under stress always remains a challenge.

COMPETITIONS

The role of competition in education is one of many controversial subjects educators have to deal with in their work. Some see it as a major motivating force, while others emphasise its damaging effects.

The essence of competing is comparing one's own performance with the performance of others and concentrating on beating those whom one sees as one's opponents. By its very nature, competing separates people from their opposition, encouraging deep-seated feelings of envy, selfishness, separateness, and the need for revenge.

The origins of competition in education can be traced to competitive sports and other kinds of games. In sports, such factors as the time one started training, the level one was at to begin with, and the progress one has made in any particular period of time, are of no consequence whatsoever. All that counts is the result: the time, the number of points, the distance. All is carefully measured, and the results are accurate and indisputable.

Is education to be similar to sports? Is it necessary to motivate children to learn by awakening in them the desire to beat their mates whom they will then see as their opponents? Is it really necessary for education to produce just a few winners and masses of losers? Is it productive to increase the level of stress in children every time they compete and fail? How much good does competition do for learning?

Like many educators, I strongly believe there are better ways to motivate children to learn. How about encouraging co-operation and non-competitive team-work? How about developing the sense of responsibility for one's own learning and helping children experience the joy of supporting others in achieving better results? Finally, how about focusing on the progress children make and treating tests merely as the necessary steps towards their ultimate goals?

Schools are under tremendous pressure to perform; my sympathy is with the teachers who have to cope with this pressure. My deepest sympathy, though, goes to those children whose lives are often destroyed, who feel losers and failures. They think it is their fault, not realising it is the system that has failed them.

My argument may have failed to convince you and, like many people, you may still believe that competition has an important part to play in educating your children. Whatever the case, I still suggest that, when working with your children, you emphasise the value of competing with oneself, i.e., measuring one's own progress. Tell your children that every time they improve their results they are the true winners.

CRITICISM

Although many people spend their lives criticising others, nobody likes it when criticism is directed at them. Pointing out other people's mistakes, wrong-doings, and unacceptable behaviour requires very special skills, particularly if what we are really aiming at is some positive outcome: improved behaviour, corrected mistakes, and generally enhanced well-being.

Think for a moment how you react to criticism.

Do you

- immediately 'hit' back?
- say nothing but feel like crying?
- think calmly about the critical comment and respond with confident politeness taking on board the other person's remarks?

And how does your child react to critical comments?

What does it depend on: the person who does it, the way in which it is done, on timing and place?

Encourage children to talk about their reactions to criticism. Point out the difference between constructive and destructive criticism.

Constructive criticism is done at the right time, at the right place, and without witnesses. It requires tact, takes into consideration the criticised person's feelings, and suggests ways of improvement. Change for the better is the primary purpose of constructive criticism.

Destructive criticism results in hurt and anger, leaving people hostile and unwilling to change.

The primary purpose here is 'getting it out of one's system' and expressing one's dissatisfaction. Seldom will permanent improvement be the result of hurtful and angry criticism.

Whether the critical comment is justified or not, we need to learn to defend ourselves against the hurt it causes. When the comment doesn't hurt so much any more, we are able to switch on thinking and either respond appropriately or learn some lessons, if appropriate, taking the critical comment into consideration...

The role of the 'Magic Armour' is to give the child time to cool down and pause before reacting in one way or another. These gained seconds are vital! When your child learns to put on the Magic Armour and breathe ten times before saying anything, he or she has mastered a skill of huge importance.

SUM IT ALL UP

How many things have we learned at school, from various courses, lectures we attended, TV programmes, or journals - only to forget about them in the two or three weeks to come? If you are like most of us, the answer is - too many...

'Sum It All Up' exercises after every section of the book are designed to prevent this from happening. Selecting five favourite exercises will require going through the whole part of the book at least once more. The chosen exercises are supposed to become a fixed part of the children's daily or weekly routine for some time to come. It does not mean, of course, that they cannot be replaced by other exercises, if the children want a change. What it does mean, however, is that only by becoming a way of life will they have a positive and permanent effect on the children's lives.

It is more advisable to choose fewer exercises or types of activities and practise them regularly than to select a large number and within a few weeks forget all about them.

loosen up

loosen up

"80 percent of learning difficulties are related to stress. Remove the stress and you remove the difficulties". [4)]

There will always be potentially stressful situations to which many children may react with tension, anxiety, or anger. I believe that the first step towards removing harmful effects of stress is the realisation that often it is not the situation itself that is stressful but the way we perceive it. Any particular situation may be extremely stressful for some, interesting, exciting, and energising for others. These are the extremes; however, there are people who will react towards a situation, which is potentially stressful for some and exciting for others, with complete indifference. It is then the question of changing our perception of certain situations, which can be done, rather than eliminating these situations from our lives, which may not be possible to do.

The second step is knowing exactly what to do in order to let go of tension in your body and to quiet your mind. We often hear people say: 'why don't you relax a little?' or 'you have to relax!'

That's all very well but for many this is an empty phrase, a meaningless suggestion. What does it mean to 'relax'? It is necessary to show children some simple but effective relaxation techniques and encourage practising them, until they become automatic responses to stress overdose.

The deep relaxation exercise (see track 1 on your companion CD) should be done every day until your child is really able to relax and until there is no more fidgeting, talking, interrupting, and getting impatient.

My experience shows that the more agitated and impatient children are, the less they will like this exercise. At the beginning children often find it boring, too long, sometimes simply silly. They complain about being uncomfortable and find it extremely difficult to keep their eyes closed. And some children flatly refuse to do it. What do we do then?!

I know I have told you earlier not to force your child to do anything. Well, we all know that putting pressure on people usually causes resentment and anger. Not good for relaxation exercises! However, I strongly recommend that despite all this, you make the biggest possible effort to convince your child to agree to go through the deep relaxation exercise, even if it means a promise of something nice happening afterwards as a reward (in case you have wondered, yes, I AM suggesting bribery!). To comfort you, let me tell you that I have not yet met a child who would not eventually give in and practically fall asleep during this exercise. It may take five to ten attempts, though, so be prepared: you may have to wait and be patient.

Some children need to lie on a soft mattress; some need a cushion, not just under their heads but also under their legs (back of the knees); still others may want to be covered with a soft blanket. Do whatever it takes to make your child as comfortable as possible.

Good luck!

Exercises

SMILING LOWERS YOUR STRESS

Many children have a great sense of humour, and it is quite easy to make them see the joke and laugh even when they are upset. Laughter is the best possible device to disperse bad feelings and lousy moods.

Make your child laugh when she/he feels angry and use this experience to talk about the role that smiling and laughter play in relaxing the body.

Jokes, amusing pictures or funny photographs never fail to improve our mood and have a wonderfully relaxing influence on us.

RELAXATION TECHNIQUES

When planning to do relaxation exercises with your child, you need to ensure that nothing and nobody will interrupt you. Close the door, draw the curtains or, if it is evening, dim the lights. Take the telephone off the hook or switch on the answering machine. Play some special relaxation tapes or some slow Baroque music on low volume (select your child's favourite Bach's music from your companion CD).

Visualisation exercises need special preparation: the first few sentences introducing the Deep Relaxation exercise on your companion CD will be a good example of what needs to be said and done.

Before you start reading the text to your child, close your eyes for a moment and breathe deeply a few times. It is of paramount importance that you feel calm and relaxed yourself.

Closing your eyes, taking a few deep breaths, dropping your shoulders and your jaw, will relax you even on a busy day.

Read the text slowly, using your soft and gentle voice, always remembering to breathe while you read. Carefully observe your child and, if necessary, adjust your reading speed to his or her needs.

When the exercise comes to an end, take care that both of you get out of the relaxed state very slowly and gently. An abrupt movement or change of the timbre of your voice can spoil the effect.

Once children know how to relax, encourage them to do these exercises every time they feel stressed, in order to develop a habit of relaxing anywhere and under any circumstances.

RELAX EVEN WHEN YOU ARE ANGRY

Anger is a powerful emotion, underneath which there is hurt, disappointment, and sadness. It is necessary for children to learn to accept their feelings and at the same time to learn how to deal constructively with strong emotions. I am talking about a skill most of us try to master for most of our lives. There are situations when we feel we are almost there, and then something happens that shows us there is still a long way to go...

I suppose that the sooner we become aware of the need to control our emotions in ways which do not harm us or anyone else, the better.

While it is important to express our emotions, children also need to know that antisocial behaviour such as hitting, spitting, yelling, and kicking, which often accompanies anger, is not acceptable.

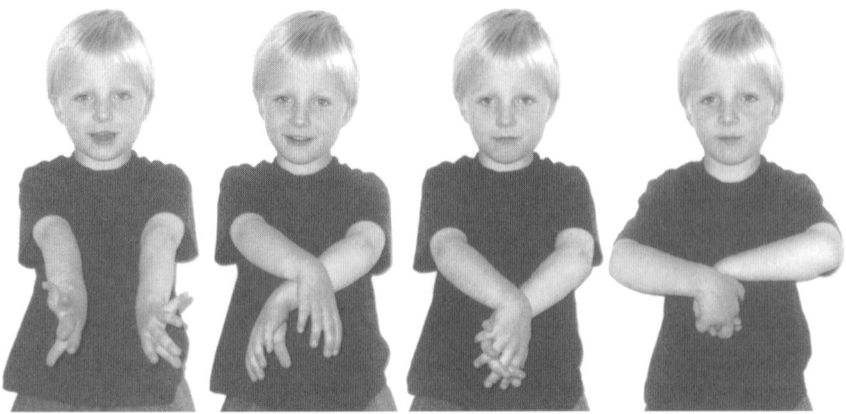

They also need to become familiar with the acceptable ways of expressing strong, troublesome emotions.

The essence of controlling anger is:

- taking time out,
- breathing deeply to calm down the heart beat,
- assuming certain postures (see photographs below) which contain the disorganised body energy and have a wonderfully soothing effect.

There is one great challenge here: when we are really angry the last thing we want is assuming some funny posture or doing a 'silly' exercise!

If your child is old enough to understand a biology lesson, tell them that when they get angry or scared, the substance called adrenaline is secreted into the blood stream. Adrenaline makes the body ready for 'fight or flight', which means that we are ready either to confront the situation or to run away. The problem is that the adrenaline in our bloodstream does one more thing: it makes clear thinking practically impossible.

It is not easy to have an angry child do an exercise. You could try doing what I often do. I make a deal with children: every time I get irritable or angry, they remind me to STOP-FREEZE and BREATHE. Whenever they get angry, I remind them to STOP-FREEZE and BREATHE. This two-way system seems to work most of the time.

On the previous page, Jack presents all the steps leading to a Hook-up, which is one of the Dennison's Brain

Gym exercises [5]. Hook-ups connect the electrical circuit in the body, containing and thus focusing both attention and disorganised energy. The mind and body relax as energy circulates through areas previously blocked by tension. This posture effectively helps the child let go of emotional stress and at the same time improves their ability to learn.

Hook-ups are extremely useful if we feel afraid of something or just nervous; they have a soothing effect on our nervous system.

DO THINGS HAVE TO STRESS YOU OUT?

Consciously or unconsciously, people make decisions about the way they see things. It is possible and very useful to become more aware of those decisions. We cannot change other people, nor do we have influence over many things that happen around us. However, we can make a choice: we can either make ourselves miserable about something that has happened to us, or we can choose to accept the fact and learn from it.

The way we interpret everything that happens to us and around us decides the way we feel. In other words, it is not the events, but what we make of them that determines whether we are stressed or not, whether we feel miserable and dissatisfied or relaxed, happy and optimistic. You can either look for the proverbial 'silver lining' and draw some lessons from the cloud, or focus on the cloud and forecast the worst storms.

I realise it sounds simplistic and over the top, but if you open your mind and think of all the difficult times in your life as important lessons, stepping-stones in your personal growth, you will probably agree with me, or at least see my point. It is easy to see the lesson a long time after the event. Rather than waiting for the passing time to show us where the lesson was, we can make an effort to see it when it is actually happening.

It is possible to change the way we see things. The exercises in this section of the book bring this to your children's attention, make them aware of the power they have over their minds and hopefully start them on the road to better, more enjoyable and less stressful lives.

Read those pages and think about the ideas before you talk about them with your child.

If, however, you see life differently, if you strongly object to the presented point of view, just let the children read the text for themselves. You may ask them what they think about it, or simply leave it without making any comments.

THE SOOTHING POWER OF MUSIC

Most of us would find it impossible to imagine the world without music. Music strongly influences our mood, while the way we feel (or want to feel!) influences the kind of music we listen to.

A certain kind of music invigorates and excites us, causes our hearts to beat faster, adds spring to our steps, and makes us want to move and dance.

Another kind of music has therapeutic qualities: much more than simply improving our mood, however important that may be, it affects our physiological condition: pulse and blood pressure decrease, the brain waves slow down and muscles relax.

There is also a kind of music, that facilitates learning. Music by Mozart has been found to have a powerful effect on the brain. American research shows that children who are exposed to a lot of Mozart's music improve their thinking skills and learn faster.

Extensive research also shows that slow Baroque music, particularly pieces by Bach, Vivaldi and Corelli, is ideal for improving learning, because its main 60-70 beats-to-the-minute pulse is identical to alpha brainwaves. It keeps your artistic (usually right) brain busy and lets your logical (left) brain focus on the task at hand. This is an ideal situation because your brain works best when both hemispheres function in harmony.

In this state of 'relaxed alertness' the brain can absorb information much faster and more effectively.

The Bach pieces on your companion CD are your beautiful learning facilitators. Play the record, close your eyes, and allow the music to take you to the most peaceful scene you can possibly imagine. Soon you will be in the state of 'relaxed alertness', the state which will make your learning more pleasant and easier to remember.

It is possible, however, that your child may need absolute silence while learning! If this is the case, let him listen to 60-70 beat-to-the-minute Baroque music before he starts learning, and later turn it off.

THE SOOTHING POWER OF NATURE

Encourage your children to enjoy contact with nature. Talk to them about all the benefits understanding nature can bring about, and teach them to respect it. Lying on the grass or a sandy beach, watching the clouds, the grass, the waves and sand grains, tree branches, leaves, and birds, may be wonderfully relaxing and truly enjoyable.

Do it together with your children, and later talk about the experience. Ask them if they have noticed something they have never seen before. Ask them to describe the shapes of clouds or leaves they have seen, ask them if they remember hearing different birdsongs.

After you have done this a few times, slowly begin to eliminate the 'activities'; your child will learn to lie down and soon 'slip' into a relaxed/meditative state and so will you, if you haven't learned this yet. You will both enjoy it, and find it extremely relaxing and energising.

SUM IT ALL UP

Follow the suggestions on page 36.

be with it

be with it

Inability to concentrate and short attention span in children are among the most common complaints of parents and teachers alike. There seem to be many disruptive children who make teachers' work extremely difficult. These are the children who appear never to listen, whose fingers always play with anything they can get hold of, who hardly ever sit still for more that a minute.

Let us look at a few aspects of our children's lives: speed-action syndrome, outdoor exercise, diet and noise pollution, and see how they influence their ability to be still and to concentrate.

Speed - action

Short attention span is the ailment of our times: for many children, texts they read have to be short and concise, the TV programmes should last no longer than 30 minutes and be packed with action. Fast speed and a quickly changing scene, both in life and in the world of mass media, a lot crammed into a very short period of time or into little space, seems to be the desired norm.

Lack of movement

Many, if not most, of our children spend practically all of their waking hours sitting: they sit at school, they sit at home doing their homework, in front of the television, in front of their computers. Parents have become unpaid taxi drivers; wherever the children go, it is always door-to-door car service. Surveys show that very few children spend enough time jumping, running around, riding bikes, or playing games in the open air.

Brain-unfriendly diet

Many children dislike vegetables and hardly ever eat fruit. Many are used to carbonated, artificially flavoured drinks, full of chemicals, sugars, and caffeine. Most don't drink enough water. If to all the 'healthy' energy foods usually enjoyed by the children, such as pasta, bread and baked beans, we add the 'unhealthy' fatty chips, sweets, chocolates, and biscuits, there is an accumulation of energy which must find an outlet.

Noise pollution

A constant background of very loud music is something many children live with on an everyday basis. Very loud music may act as an 'energizer', as well as like a psychotic drug, but it does not create an environment necessary to concentrate on something other than listening to the music. Listening to very loud music through headphones may have a damaging effect on the child's brain and hearing.

Before we see our children as Attention Deficit Disorder sufferers, let us try to introduce them to drinking more still water and eating more vegetables. Let us try to ensure they spend time on outdoor play. Let us also make an effort to reduce their sugar and caffeine intake, and cut down on the hours spent in front of the computer and watching TV. All this appears to be tough measures, but if you seriously want to help your child improve their concentration, you will need to be tough.

We have been brought up to believe that in order to pay attention and learn children have to sit up, not move, and look at the speaker. No doubt children who behave this way are the easiest and most pleasant audience. However, with all the research into multi-sensory learning, the role of movement in learning, and the different learning styles, we now know that to tell some children to sit still and look at the teacher is as if we were saying to them: *Don't' learn!*

Next time your children swing their legs, play with their fingers or a marble, look at the ceiling or at the floor while you talk to them, don't automatically assume they are not paying attention to your words! They may be auditory and kinaesthetic learners who need to move, manipulate objects and turn their dominant ears to you, in order to learn.

Exercises

FOCUSING YOUR SENSES

Every time you do a visualisation with your child, I recommend you take some time to 'set the scene'. You need to create a perfect ambience necessary for the visualisation to be effective.

Get yourself into a calm, relaxed mood: put one hand on your heart, the other on your navel and breathe slowly a few times. Put on a tape with relaxation music or some slow Baroque music (see your companion CD); you may prefer silence, so do what feels best.

Dim bright lights, or draw the curtains.

Close the door, and ask anybody who is in the house to make as little noise as possible. If you can, take the telephone off the hook.

Prepare thick blankets or sleeping bags, some cushions to put under the child's head and knees, and some light blankets to cover with, if necessary.

Read the exercises slowly, using your soft and gentle voice, giving your child plenty of time to internalise the suggestions and follow them. Observe the children carefully, and be sensitive to everything that is happening in them.

Towards the end of the visualisation, your child will be 'in a different world', a 'spaced out' state. It is important that the return to this world happens gently and slowly.

Say for example:

now start stretching...

stretch your arms...

your legs...

stretch... stretch...

turn slowly to your side...

breathe... breathe...

cover your eyes with your palms

and open them...

when you feel you are ready

slowly, very slowly sit up...

Talk about the exercise with the children. Ask them how they felt, what they saw, and whether they enjoyed the exercise. If they did not, ask what upset them or what went wrong with the exercise.

Children who are nervous, impatient, and 'wriggly', may not enjoy visualisation exercises. Do persevere! Try again, and again, maybe ask someone else to do the exercises with your child. Eventually most children learn to enjoy them and get better and better at relaxation and visualisation. The benefits are enormous, so it is worth the effort.

BRAIN BUTTONS

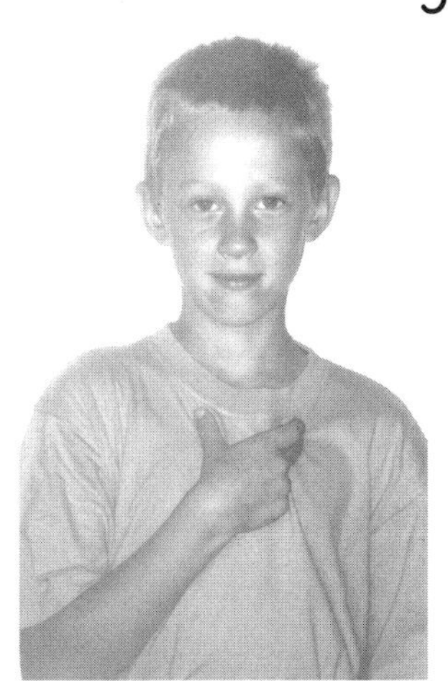

Brain Buttons belong to Dennison's Brain Gym exercises.

By pressing and massaging the small indentations under the collarbone, we stimulate the carotid arteries that supply freshly oxygenated blood to the brain. Once the brain gets a supply of oxygen, our attention, thinking and vision improves.

HELICOPTER SPIN

Spinning around in one direction wakes up the brain and prepares it for new information. It requires balance and stimulates the vestibular system, an important component of the brain's ability to maintain alertness. The vestibular system is a sensory-motor system, connecting the canals of the inner ear - brain stem - eyes - core muscles.

Spinning has been a part of some famous rituals; the Huns and the Whirling Dervishes, among others, have been known to spin to experience a specific state of mind. Prof. Lyelle Palmer introduced spinning as an exercise improving the learning ability of children [6)].

Tell the children simply to spread their arms and spin clockwise (following their right arm) 15 times.

When they stop, have them join fingertips of both hands and look at their fingers (see photograph on the previous page) until they no longer feel dizzy. Repeat the cycle up to three times.

> A word of caution here:
>
> Always protect your children from hurting themselves, as they can easily lose their balance. Some people may find spinning unpleasant. If you observe any unwanted side effects or are aware of an existing medical condition, please consult your doctor.

WALKING WITH YOUR EYES WIDE OPEN AND YOUR EARS WELL TUNED

Go shopping with your children, and let them choose for themselves little notebooks.

They will need them when they go for the 'adventure walk' with you. It is also possible to do the listening part of the exercise at home. Sit quietly, and tell the children to listen to different sounds: a knock, the phone next door, a bird, their own breath, the floor creaking, a dog in the street, an aeroplane, etc., etc.

A well-known game of taking objects out of the bag blindfolded and guessing what they are is another focus exercise. You can make it quite tricky by choosing similar yet different objects, e.g. a large orange and a small grapefruit.

BUTTERFLY'S WINGS

The original name of this Brain Gym exercise is 'Lazy 8's'. Drawing the sign of infinity (an eight lying on its side) enables the child to cross the visual body midline and activates both right and left eyes, integrating the right and left visual fields.

This is an extremely useful exercise. When practised regularly, it enables the child to read without reversing or changing places of letters.

THE CRANE

The original name of this Brain Gym exercise is 'The Elephant'. In this exercise it is important that the whole body moves together: the trunk, the head and the arm are all one.

This exercise activates the inner ear for improved balance and integrates both hemispheres of the brain for listening with both ears. It releases tight neck and shoulder muscles.

YOUR FOCUS SUPPORTERS

Touch is an extremely important sense for many of us, and yet we often discourage children from holding little objects, like pebbles or conkers, and playing with them while reading, thinking, or talking.

If touch is important for your child, encourage her or him to find some favourite little objects and put them in their pockets. Holding a familiar and pleasant object may reduce nervousness and improve thinking.

LISTENING WITH ALL YOUR HEART

Take the time and invite your children to make a few pairs of red felt 'heart-ears' with you. Felt is better than paper because it is soft, warm, and doesn't tear easily.

The 'heart-ears' are essential for this exercise. If the children are in the right kind of mood, putting the 'heart-ears' on their ears brings about a magical transformation. Treat the 'heart-ears' as something very special, maybe a little mysterious...Tell the children the heart-ears are there to connect their ears with their hearts, to make their listening caring and sympathetic.

If the children appear to be in a 'fooling around' mood, let them play for a while and then put the heart-ears away. Maybe the next time you do the exercise the mood will change.

You can make use of the heart-ears every time you want to say something important to your children. Before you begin talking, ask them to put the heart-ears on. Also, when your children want you to listen to them really attentively, they may ask you to put on your heart-ears. This will give both of you a good chance to become better listeners.

FIXING YOUR ATTENTION ON THE PAGE

This exercise may be done with any text, and most children find it very amusing.

Give the children a signal to start, and ask them to keep circling the letters, not stopping even for a moment, until they come to the end of the text. The purpose of this exercise is for the children to keep their eyes on the page and along the lines for a considerable length of time.

If your children have a short attention span, you may start by giving them shorter texts written in large print. Gradually make the texts longer and the print smaller.

Looking for and circling all the letters appearing in the child's first name has a chance of engaging all children, including those having serious difficulties with focusing attention.

SUM IT ALL UP

For suggestions see page 36.

the way you learn best

the way you learn best

The fact that everybody learns in a different way is probably the most important thing to know for learners and teachers alike. Although our learning styles may differ dramatically, we are taught as if we all learned in one way. A mismatch between our preferred learning style and the way we are taught frequently results in very poor progress. It is very likely that a certain percentage of children classified as 'special needs' are simply those who have not been taught in the way they can learn.

Anybody who has ever taught a class of thirty children knows that in such a group each child's individual, unique needs cannot possibly be met. This is why it becomes a necessity to involve parents in educating their children.

As a parent-teacher-educator, bear in mind that:

- if your children are not making progress, it is likely that they are not taught in a way which makes it possible for them to learn, in other words that the wrong learning profile is being addressed (e.g., the child may be a visual/kinaesthetic, right brain, right eye and right ear dominant learner, and be taught as if he or she were auditory, left brain, right eye and left ear dominant. Two totally different learning profiles!);

- it is critical to guide your children towards discovering what their preferred learning style is. It is also critical to find out how children can help themselves when they are taught in ways different from their preferred learning style.

Exercises

WHY DO WE LEARN ?

Thinking about the reasons we learn is a part of your child's discovery process.

It is also important because the reasons we learn influence the attitude towards learning and, thus, the results.

Encourage your child to be specific when filling the bare branches.

Here is an example of how this could be done:

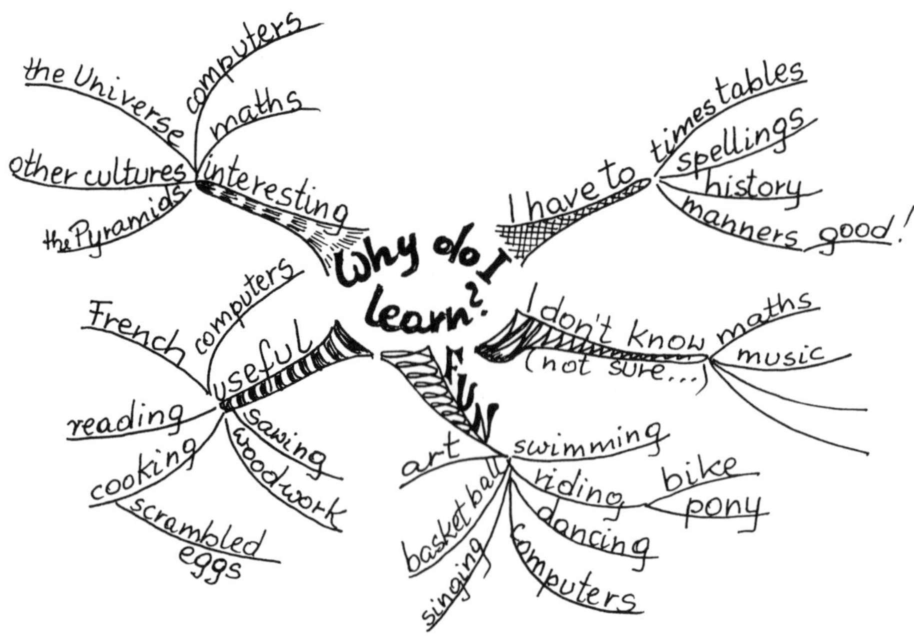

It is sometimes tempting to correct children's responses and to tell them what they *should* (!) find interesting. What works much better is accepting that every answer the child gives is correct.

YOU ARE BORN WITH A PASSION FOR LEARNING

If your child needs some help to complete this exercise, gently prompt:

1. Some things we learn without or with little help from others:
   walking, talking, riding a bike, playing football, eating
   with knife & fork, playing hop-scotch, playing computer games, doing roly-poly and cart wheels...
2. The ways in which we learn those things:
   trying over and over again (not giving up!),
   observing people, adults or children, and being copy-cats,
   figuring it out for yourself,
   asking somebody to show you how to do it,
   following instructions in a book / manual.

Talk with the children about something they learned by trying over and over again and never giving up until they did it. Ask them if they remember any other thing they, or somebody they know, have learned this way.

Talk about the value of perseverance. Tell the children about something you, or somebody you know, have learned thanks to persevering. You may also make up an interesting story, illustrating the idea, if no real life examples come to mind.

HOW DID YOU / WILL YOU LEARN THESE ?

All the answers the children give are correct. It is not always easy, but try to stop yourself from correcting your child's answers or suggesting changes. You may wish to tell your child how YOU learned those things and discuss it with your child, comparing the different ways people learn.

Children are often surprised to discover how many things they have already learned all by themselves or with very little help from others. Realising that it was their own effort and determination empowers them for taking on responsibilities for new learning.

The learner is the central and the only indispensable part of learning. The best books, wonderfully interesting films, great teachers, or most sophisticated computers can do absolutely nothing, unless the child wants to learn.

This also is an empowering thought and a realisation essential to creating life-long, independent learners.

YOUR MOST IMPORTANT SENSE

This exercise awakens in children the awareness about the role our senses play in learning. It also encourages self-observation, which will lead them to discovering their own, individual ways of learning.

LEARNING SOMETHING BY HEART

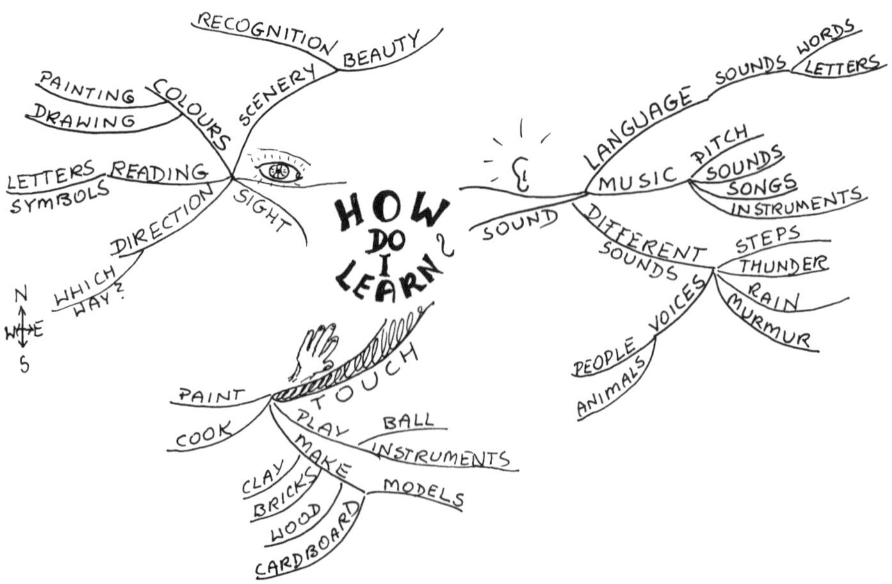

As in previous exercises, there are no right or wrong answers: every answer your child gives is correct. Remind the children that there may well be more than one answer to each question.

It is possible that working with the exercises presents a big challenge. After all, the questions will make them think about something they have probably never thought about before. Don't worry that some questions may remain unanswered. Whatever the outcome, the exercise will make the children aware of the many possibilities and choices they can make. This is already a lot. Let it be enough for the time being.

DISCOVER HOW YOU LEARN BEST

These two exercises summarise the choices children have when learning something.

When you look carefully at the two pages, you will see that the two exercises are almost identical in content; what differs is the format. What the first exercise does in the traditional, multiple-choice form, the other does in the form of radiant notes.

Previous pages have already introduced the children to radiant notes, called Mind Maps by their originator, Tony Buzan [7)]. There will be more examples of mind maps, before the mechanism of making them is explained. It has been my intention to introduce the children to radiant notes in an informal way, to let them get used to the novelty, and only then to teach them how they can make such notes for themselves.

YOUR INCREDIBLY AMAZING BRAIN

If you feel that your child is ready to learn about the brain and would find it interesting, ask him or her to read the text for themselves. Ask them a few questions, and gently probe whether they have understood the text.

If you think your children may find reading this text boring, read it yourself first, and then TELL them a 'Brain Story'. Find a picture of the brain and some fascinating information about it in an encyclopaedia or some other book, and make your 'story' as interesting and exciting as possible.

After all, the brain is truly the most exciting thing imaginable!

THE RIGHT OR THE LEFT HEMISPHERE ?

In order to establish the child's learning profile, and on that basis to be able to suggest the most effective learning strategies, we need to find out which hemisphere, eye, ear, hand, and foot are dominant in your child.

Determining the dominant eye, ear, hand, or foot, is relatively easy. However, it is quite a challenge to establish which of your child's hemispheres is the dominant one.

Is it the right one, also called *artistic* or *Gestalt*, or the left one, known as the *science* or the *logic* hemisphere?

This exercise will not make it possible for you to establish with absolute certainty which is your child's dominant hemisphere. It will, however, give you and your children some understanding of how the two hemispheres function and point you in the direction of the probable dominance.

If your children find the questions bewildering, leave this and the next exercise for the time being. Come back to the questions at some later stage when you feel the children are ready for them.

USING YOUR RIGHT HEMISPHERE

Whether or not the previous exercises suggest that your child's right brain is dominant, I recommend that you try doing with him or her all the exercises in this section.

These exercises are useful for every learner. While showing the right-brain dominant children that it's not only alright but desirable for them to move, touch, use lots of colour and start reading from the end of the book (things they may have been told not to do), they show the left-brainers how they can activate their right brain for better balance and better results.

Introduce the suggested way of learning slowly, over a few days, even weeks. They have to be tried out and practised a number of times before they can become firmly established learning habits.

THIS IS THE WAY I LEARN BEST

This exercise reinforces all the discoveries children have made so far about their preferred ways of learning. It encourages self-awareness and the sense of responsibility for their own learning.

The purpose of all the self-awareness exercises is shifting the focus

from the **teacher** to the **learner**,

from *I am being taught* to *I am learning.*

ACTIVATING YOUR NEGLECTED HEMISPHERE

Many of us avoid doing things, which appear to be difficult and require from us a great deal of effort and patience. Perseverance and determination are often in short supply, and we give up easily, sometimes even before we have had a chance to find out what exactly the apparent difficulty is.

Those of us who have strong dominance of one or the other hemisphere often have a lot of resistance towards activities that seemingly 'belong' to the other brain and appear to be almost 'unnatural' to us.

Do not push too hard; try gently steering your child towards those activities, showing no irritation or annoyance and being always prepared to back off.

Forcing children to do anything results in immediate resistance, which in turn causes stress. Learning under these conditions is not only a waste of time and energy but also discouraging and harmful.

CROSS PAT AND CROSS WALK

Given the name of Cross Crawl by Dr. Dennison, this is yet another of the Brain Gym exercises. Cross Crawl activates both hemispheres of the brain, making learning easier.

This is one of the most important exercises children ought to do every day. Get them into the habit of doing it regularly.

Cross Crawl activates the brain for crossing the visual/auditory/kinaesthetic/tactile midline, for left-to-right eye movements, and for improved both eye vision.

YOUR MANY INTELLIGENCES

Professor Howard Gardner of Harvard University is the author of the theory of multiple intelligences [8)]. He maintains that rather than just 'an intelligence', we have at least seven types of intelligences.

Here is a short description of the many intelligences which work for us:

Linguistic intelligence

> sensitive to language patterns, likes to read and write, good speller, likes word-games, may be a good public speaker

Logical-mathematical intelligence

> likes abstract thinking and problem solving, is well organised, prefers orderly notes, enjoys computers

Visual-spatial intelligence

> thinks in pictures, likes drawing, painting and sculpturing, easily reads maps, charts and diagrams, remembers in pictures and has a colour sense

Musical intelligence

sensitive to the emotional power of music, to pitch, rhythm and timbre, likes playing an instrument or singing

Bodily-kinaesthetic intelligence

good control of body movements, good timing and reflexes, likes to engage in sports, likes to touch, good in handicrafts, sensitive to physical environment, fidgety, mechanically minded

Interpersonal (social) intelligence

relates well to people, able to read other's intentions, enjoys being with people, communicates well, enjoys group activities, may manipulate

Intrapersonal (intuitive) intelligence

sensitive to own values and purpose in life, aware of own feelings, strengths and weaknesses, able to access 'inner self'

Emotional intelligence

able to value the role of emotions, to accept emotions as well as control them, capable of expressing emotions in non-destructive way

Most teaching addresses our linguistic and logical-mathematical intelligences. Those are the intelligences determining exam results, grades, and the child's academic future. While it is good and necessary to develop these, it is also necessary for children to know that:

- all intelligences are at least as important in life as the linguistic and mathematical ones,
- everybody is intelligent, because everybody has some of the eight intelligences developed,
- it is possible to improve any of your intelligences, if you choose to do so.

It is important that all children understand and remember the three points made above.

The children with well-developed linguistic and mathematical intelligences will learn to appreciate and value others who seem to be lacking in those particular areas, understanding that they are intelligent in a different way. Children whose school intelligences are not very well activated will have the understanding that they are also intelligent and creative and will learn to value their diverse potential. However, in order to be successful in their academic work, the latter will have to improve their 'school' intelligences, too...

MORE ABOUT YOUR INTELLIGENCES

We all know people who did badly at school and yet managed to become successful in life. And yet very often, most unnecessarily, they carry with them the notion of being 'school fools' for the rest of their lives. Some people manage to get over the school failures and live happy and successful live. There are those, however, who never fully recover their confidence and whose self-esteem is damaged for life.

Now that we are aware of multiple intelligences, this should not be happening to anybody any more.

YOU BODY LANGUAGE AND LEARNING

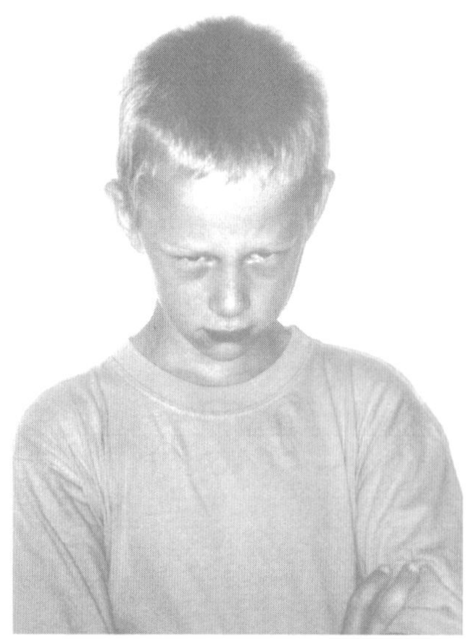

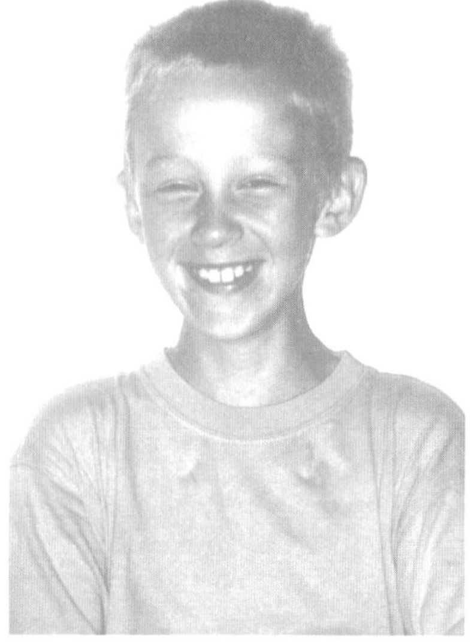

Children find this exercise very amusing. It is a joke, but not only that. It shows them that their body language has a big influence on the way they feel.

Two conclusions may be drawn from this exercise:

- if they are not feeling on top of the world, their bodies can help them feel better;
- trying to learn or doing anything else with 'miserable' body language has small chance of bringing success.

SEND YOUR BRAIN ON HOLIDAY

Breaks are essential!

Trying to work when we are very tired and pushing ourselves beyond our limits is never very productive. Some people need more frequent breaks than others. Help your children become sensitive to their mind/body needs by allowing them to decide when they want to have breaks.

During their breaks, encourage them to drink water, move around, dance, do Brain Gym and breathing exercises.

NOURISH YOU BRAIN

Things good for the brain:

- oxygen,
- water,
- good thoughts,
- vegetables, fruit, fish, pasta, nuts.

Tell your child to make a colourful poster and put it up on the wall for everyone to remember what the brain really needs!

SUM IT ALL UP

Follow the suggestions on page 36.

your

magic learning tools

your magic learning tools

It is difficult to imagine the world without computers, mobile phones, the Internet, not to mention cameras or washing machines. People did live without all these gadgets until quite recently, but not many of us choose to be without them now.

Until recently, we knew very little about the way our brains work. Thanks to a vast amount of fascinating research, we now know a little more. With the knowledge about the brain came some brilliant learning tools, many of which are still waiting to become generally acknowledged, appreciated, and used.

Why be without them if they are available and can make learning so much easier and so much more fun?

Exercises in the book will make you acquainted with some of these tools. They probably will seem strange, and using them may be uncomfortable at first. After all, you have been used to other ways of learning for quite some time now. Do your best not to be easily discouraged and persevere.

I promise you that you will not regret it!

Exercises

I HAVE TO READ THIS. VERY WELL, BUT WHAT FOR ?

Let the children think and give their own answers to the question above before they see the mind map on the next page.

Show the children how they can read the mind map. Here is an example of how this may be done:

Why do we read? I can think of five main reasons. We read when we need to ***learn*** *something, when we prepare for tests or exams. We read for* ***pleasure****, such things as novels, stories, comics, as well as letters from friends or enjoyable articles in magazines. For some of us reading is a* ***habit****: we read everything we lay our hands on, wherever we are. We read to practise reading when we want to become more* ***fluent*** *readers, to improve our reading speed and comprehension. We often read because we want to* ***find information*** *we need in newspapers and encyclopaedias, in recipe books, timetables, instruction manuals, in magazines, or on the Internet.*

DIFFERENT WAYS YOU READ

This exercise is for children who are already pretty fluent readers and who need to be made aware of the different ways of reading.

If your children are still slow readers, leave it for a while and come back to it, when the time is right.

The answers suggesting how the texts can be read will depend on the children's ability to read and comprehend.

Here are some possible suggestions:

- A magazine article that interests you
  - not very fast, paying attention to detail
- A letter from your best friend
  - pretty fast and maybe twice to add to the fun

- A chapter in your geography book
  - first browse through the chapter, then read marking the important information, then read again
- Some information in the encyclopaedia or on the Internet
  - browse through the text fishing out the important bits
- A time table
  - browse through the text
- An entertainment guide
  - browse through the text
- A novel
  - probably not very fast, enjoying the fun
- Your own essay
  - not very fast, paying attention to details (introducing changes and corrections)

The reading speed and the way we read differs from person to person. It doesn't really matter how children choose to read letters from friends, novels or entertainment guides. It is, however, important that they learn how to read when they want to learn and remember what they have read. The next ten pages will teach them how to do it.

BEFORE YOU START READING

Put together 5 - 10 different books: a novel, a selection of poems, an encyclopaedia, a book of exercises, a book about the Tudors, about horses, dancing, mountain climbing, football teams, anything that might interest your children.

Tell the children to read the titles, subtitles, names of the authors, and the blurbs. Then tell them to look at pictures, photographs, tables, and things written in bold or coloured print. Finally, have them read a few sentences from the beginning and a few sentences from the end of the book.

Ask the children how well, in their opinion, they know the books now.

YOUR NEW TEXTBOOK - GETTING ACQUAINTED

This exercise is a continuation of the previous one. This time the children will probably need no more than gentle reminders of what to do next while getting acquainted with their books.

Tell your children that becoming familiar with the book before they actually start reading will help them read faster, understand better, and remember more.

This preparation for reading is extremely effective for all children; however, it is indispensable for children with strong right brain dominance.

MAKING FRIENDS WITH YOUR TEXTBOOK

Let each child choose one of the books they have become acquainted with, sit down comfortably and close their eyes. Read the exercise text very slowly, pausing at the end of every line.

At the end, ask the children to repeat after you:

You are interesting, easy to understand and fun to read.

Ask them to say it again, until you hear them say it with genuine conviction.

WHAT YOU SEE ON THE PAGE

Write on an A4 sheet of paper in bold print any sentence you wish, circle one or two letters in the middle of the sentence, and guide your children through the exercise.

Many children see better and read more fluently when they hold the book in their hands, in an upright position. Let your children try it out, and ask them whether they have found reading this way easier. If not, leave them to find their best position for themselves.

YOU COULD SEE MORE

Most people's eye muscles don't get enough exercise. This is because the eyes move very little when we read, watch television, or use the computer, which is what many of us do for hours every day.

This eye exercise helps expand the peripheral (sideways) vision and will enable your child to take in 3 - 5+ words at a time. It will, therefore, be advantageous for both: your children's vision and their reading fluency.

YOUR LITTLE HELPERS: A FINGER, A PENCIL, A RULER

For years, many of us were told that using a finger or a pencil while reading reduces the reading speed.

New research assures us that using pointers does the exact opposite: it increases our reading speed. The eyes of an unskilled reader tend to wander all over the page, making a lot of jerky movements. Pointers help the eyes focus on the words and move smoothly along the lines. If your children feel comfortable using pointer while reading, encourage them to do so. There is no need, however, to insist that all children use pointers. If your children are happy reading without them, let them be.

READING IS A WONDERFUL THING TO DO

Children find it easier to develop a reading habit when someone who genuinely likes reading does it with them.

It is possible that with all the work you have to do you don't find the time to do much reading yourself.

I suggest you try doing it on holidays, when everyone is more relaxed and when there is less pressure to be in bed at a certain time.

Go to bed with a book, and encourage your children to do the same, even if only to look at some pictures and read a few words. Provide them with a good choice of books, and always let them choose the book they want to read. If you do it regularly, there is a good chance your children will soon become bookworms!

HOW TO READ

This is how you may read the mind map to/with your children.

*Reading is meant to be a **pleasure.***

*We read **2,3,4** or more **words at a time**. People who are not very fluent readers or those with poor sight, like **large print** (although I wear glasses, I still prefer larger print!)*

*It is all right to use **'helpers' such as a finger**, a pencil, or a ruler to guide us along the lines. It also helps to hold the book in an **upright position**, at an appropriate distance.*

*Everyone needs to find their **favourite body position** for reading. Some people like lying on the floor or a sofa. Others prefer to sit at the table, on the bed, on a cushion; still others read best when standing! Any position is good, as long as it works for you.*

*Covering the text with a **coloured transparent plastic sheet** can improve your reading speed. People need to choose their favourite colour by trying them out while reading. (It is possible you don't want any colour, and that's fine, too.)*

*Reading **aloud** may help you remember the text better. If it is necessary for you to remember what you are reading, you may record the text and later listen to it while walking, playing a ball, or even washing up!*

*To practice reading, choose books that are **interesting** for you. Practice will make your reading fluent, easy, and fun!*

You may notice that I have added a few details that do not appear on the map. A mind map is a flexible device, and any additional number of branches may be added at any time.

LETTERS: BIG OR SMALL ?

Until you see that your children enjoy reading and don't need any more encouragement in this matter, select for them books with large print. In the initial stages it certainly minimises the effort and maximises the fun.

HOW TO READ SO THAT YOU CAN REMEMBER

Prepare a few short and interesting texts from books or

magazines for the children to choose from. Ideally, they should be about something the children, for some reason, want to remember.

Once the children have selected six texts for themselves, tell them to read the first text and mark the important information with coloured markers. With the second text, ask them to follow the second suggestion, with the third text the third suggestion, and so on. The order in which they do it has no significance.

Completing the exercise may take a long time, maybe even a few days.

Do the exercise a few times with different texts, each time following the six suggested ways to remember the information. When you think they have done enough practice, ask the children to select their favourite way to remember what they have read. The awareness of all the possibilities, as well as the practised favourite way, will prove extremely useful and hopefully effective when preparing for tests and exams.

REMEMBER, REMEMBER

This exercise tells the children what more they can do to remember what they have learned.

Select an article from a children's magazine, an interesting report from someone's travels, or any other text you think your children may find interesting. Read it to the children and later see what they remember. Then talk to them about all the memorable details, trying to figure out with them what made them remember those things:

- Were they unexpected and surprising, or very interesting?
- Did they appear at the beginning, or at the end of the text?
- Did they remind them of something they had already known or heard about?
- Was it easy to imagine them?
- Were they repeated a few times in the text?

Repeat this exercise, using a different text every time. Then combine it with the previous ('How to read...') exercise. Once the children have practised the ways of memorising information, preparing for tests and exams will become infinitely easier.

WORDS FLOW SWIFTLY... STRAIGHT ONTO PAPER

The purpose of this exercise is learning to deal with the phenomenon known as 'writer's block'.

It consists in suspending all judgement, i.e. writing without evaluating whether what you are writing is good or bad. Accept that 'anything goes' and write down anything that comes to your head. It sounds like a silly little thing to do but I recommend you try it with the children: it unlocks the flow of ideas and removes barriers built by the critical mind.

Because it looks silly and playful, it also has a chance to reduce dramatically the paralysing fear of making mistakes.

I suggest you treat it as a game and do it with your children when there is no pressure of any homework or project deadline. Just fun.

Practised a number of times, this may turn out to be a permanent solution to your child's writing inhibitions.

BRIEF OR ELABORATE ?

Treat this exercise as a game you can play in the car, waiting for a dentist appointment, or just sitting in the garden and sipping lemonade. The task is to ask all the possible questions about a given topic. How many questions can we all think of?

Here are some topic ideas:

My favourite team lost the game.

Last night I had a dream.

There will be a birthday party next week.

Two of the most important things people can't live without are water and love.

Ask everybody to write as many questions about the sentence as they possibly can.

This is not a competition. See how many sentences are similar and how many are completely different. Let everybody add other people's questions to their lists.

When children get used to asking questions about any given topic, they will always have plenty of ideas to write about.

WRITING TELLS A STORY

Children have wonderful imagination but often decide, consciously or unconsciously, not to use it for their schoolwork. Their judgmental minds take over and tell them that imagination is 'fun stuff', not good for serious things.

Play some soothing and relaxing music, and tell the children to lie down comfortably and close their eyes. Ask them to imagine some lovely scenery, a beautiful place where they have already been, either in real life or in their imagination. Tell them to see it very clearly, to hear the sounds and smell the smells of the place. Slowly, very slowly bring them back to the room. When they are ready, tell them to write in detail what they have experienced, to draw a picture or write a poem.

Another possibility is to tell the children where to 'go' in their imagination and later describe what they have experienced.

Suggested topics may also give your children a number of possibilities of what to write about.

If you succeed in making it fun, you may end up with a good number of compositions that could then be made into a book.

A few suggestions:

- let children use their imagination and show your appreciation for it;
- let children choose their topics for themselves or give them topics to choose from, if they don't come up with their own;
- do not criticise handwriting, do not immediately correct spelling or grammatical mistakes. Constant criticism most certainly puts people off writing!

Type all the compositions (without any errors!) and print them out.

Bind them into a book and ask the children to draw pictures and to design cover pages for their books.

Few things are as inspiring as seeing one's name in print!

HOW TO SPELL THIS WORD ?

The use of colour, touch, the Brain Gym exercises, and the movement of hand and arm together are the potential 'helpers' in learning ‘spellings’.

Use large sheets of paper, ideally flip chart size A1. Ask the children to choose their favourite colour finger paints and let them copy their ‘spellings’ with two or three fingers, painting large size letters. Let them copy the same word two or three times.

Then write neatly the words yourself, one word per sheet, and mount them on the wall. Ask the children to make a pretend camera lens from their fingers (see the photograph) and focalise on one word at a time. Tell the children that the fingers and eyes are their lenses, that the brain is their film, and, 'click', have them take a photograph. The word stays on their film, i.e. in their brain.

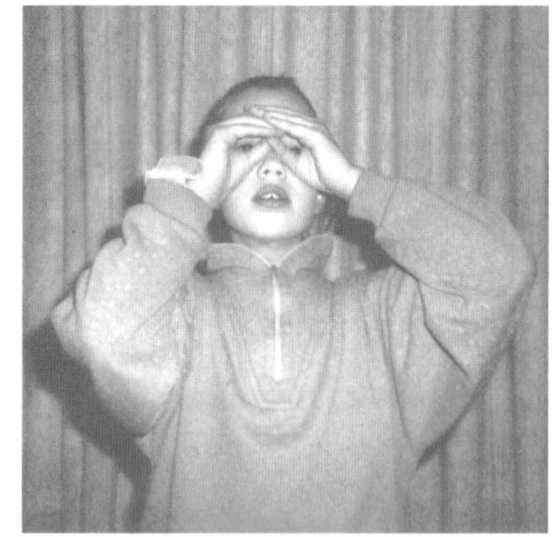

You would be amazed if you knew how many children have improved their spelling using their pretend finger cameras!

ON THE LINES OR RADIANTLY ? (Tony Buzan’s Mind Mapping)

Those pages tell you everything you need to know at that stage about this wonderful learning tool.

To find out more about Mind Mapping, see recommended reading list on page 93.

MY SCHOOL

Children who are educated at home and do not go to school can make a mind map about a club, a centre, or any other place they know well.

One of many possibilities to complete the mind map:

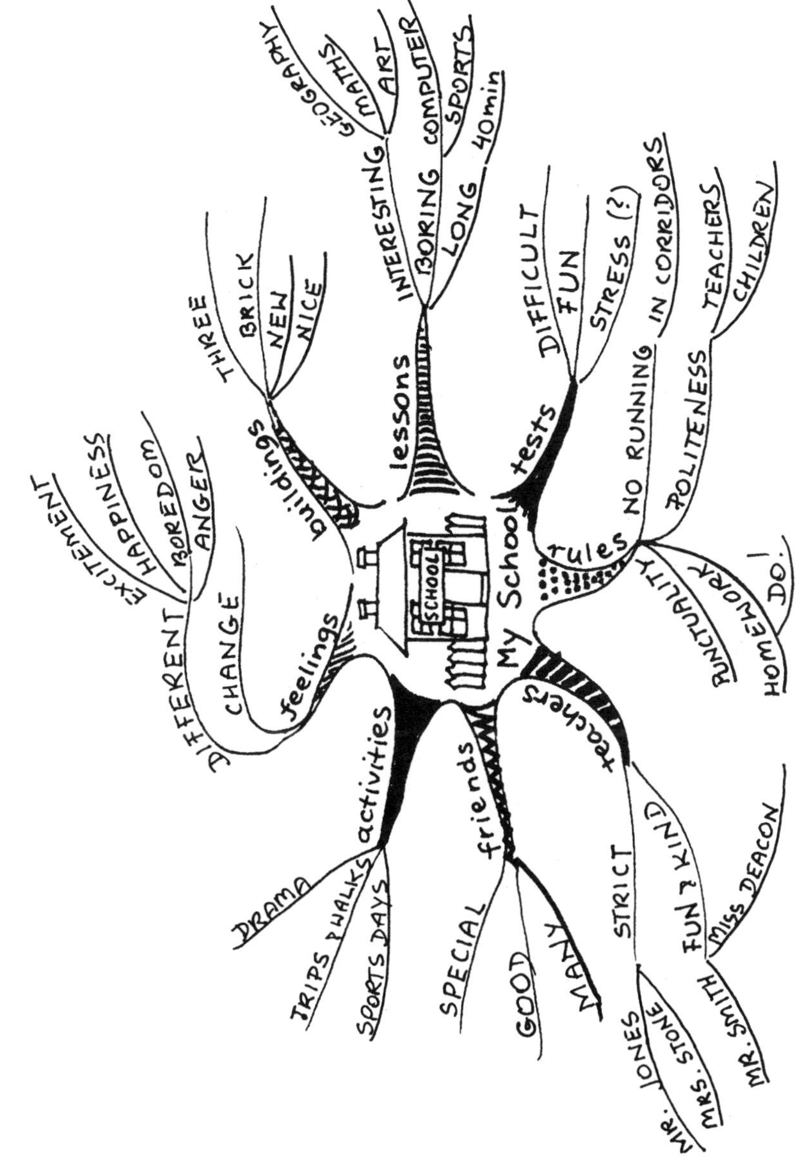

MIND-NOTES AND HEART-NOTES

One of many possibilities to complete the mind maps:

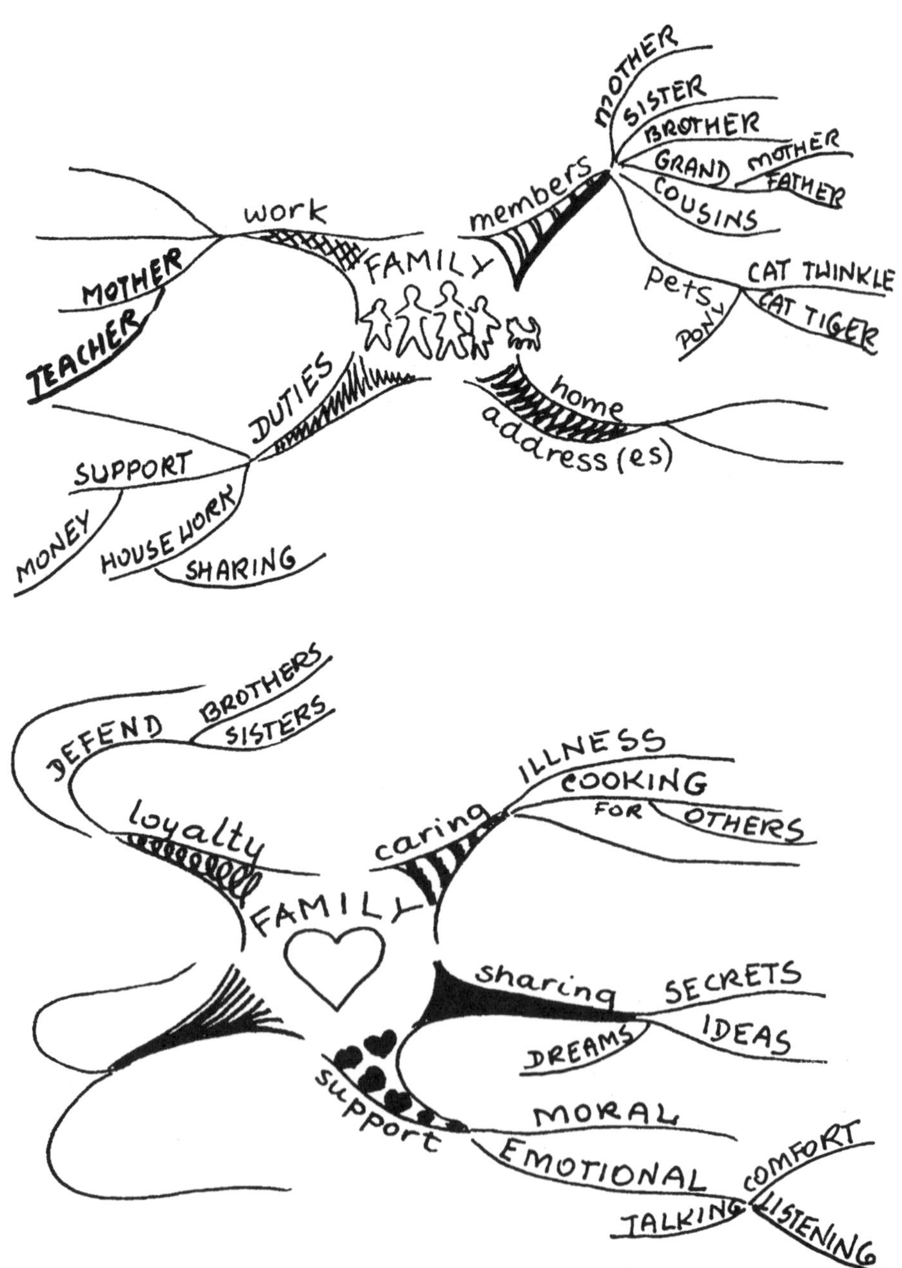

FROM RADIANT NOTES TO AN ESSAY

One child's mind map and the first two paragraphs of her composition.

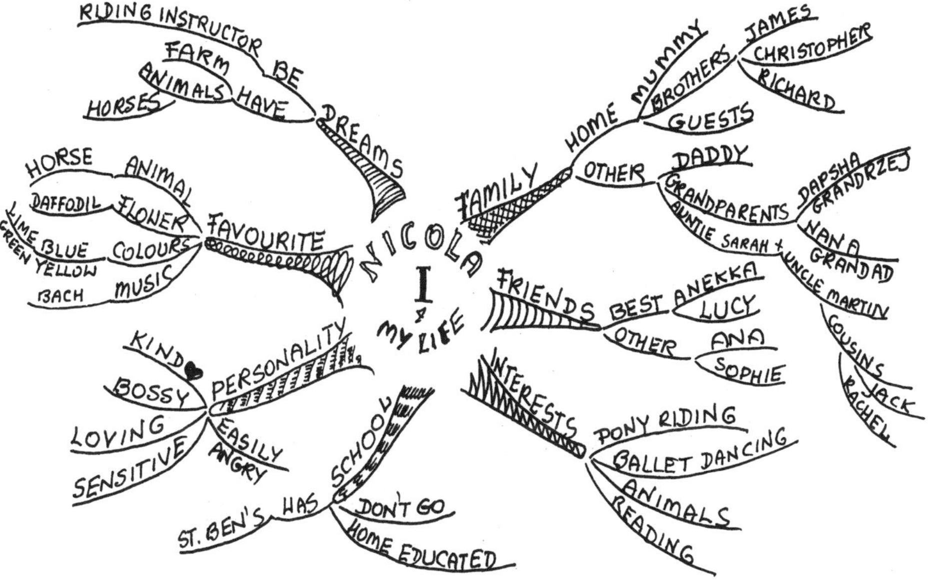

My name is Nicola and I am 10 years old. I live with my Mummy and my three younger brothers in a house which has three bedrooms upstairs and two rooms downstairs. I have other members in my family: my Daddy, my Grandparents, Aunties, Uncles and my cousins. Of all the cousins I have I only visit Jack and Rachel.

My best friend's name is Anekka but I also have others friends, Lucy, Ana and Sophie. I play with them a lot and quarrel with them, too.

Of all the things I do I like pony riding best. I love riding so much that I could ride every day and never have enough. I love all animals and I read many books about them and watch programmes on television about them. Another thing I like is dancing, I haven't danced for some time now but Mummy said I could go to ballet lessons again in September.

TRANSFORMING A STORY INTO RADIANT NOTES

Here is an example of how a story can be presented in the form of a mind map:

Here is an example of radiant notes one child made, preparing for a science test:

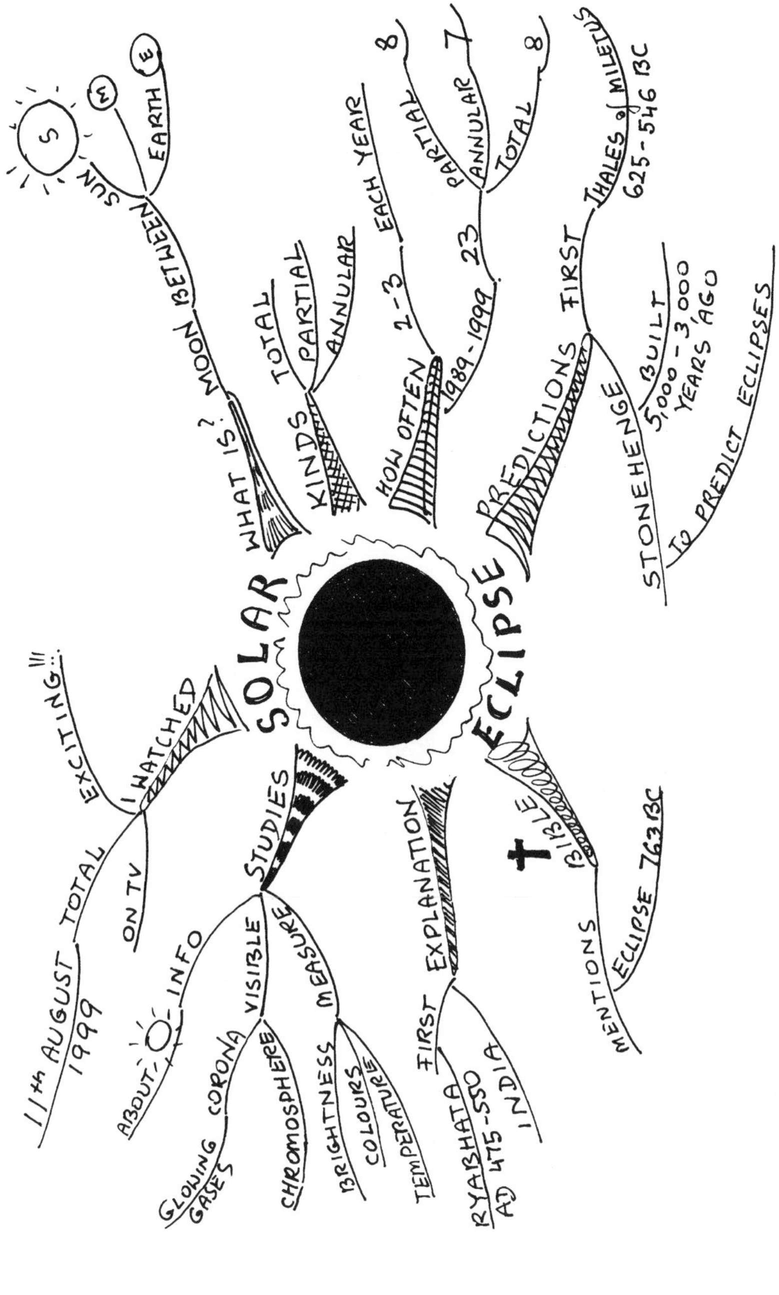

SUM IT ALL UP

Follow suggestions on page 36.

the closing exercise

Ask you children to browse through their files and find their five *SUM IT ALL UP* radiant notes sheets, each representing their favourite exercises from one of the sections of the workbook.

Get a large sheet of paper, ideally A2 or even A1, and ask the children to copy all the information from the smaller notes onto the large one, and this way make a clear, colourful, and pretty *Reminder Map*.

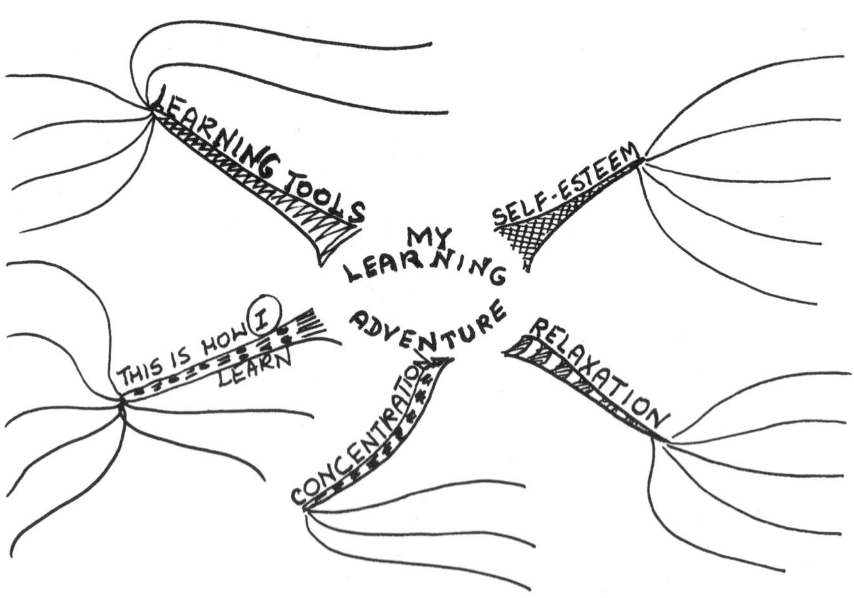

If your children haven't made the *SUM IT ALL UP* notes, don't let it bother anyone. Just browse together with your children through the book and together identify their favourite exercises. Then make a *Reminder Map*, as suggested above.

Here is an additional exercise to join the big reminder map on your child's bedroom wall.

Let the child's teacher, parent, grandparent, or best friend add to this mind map their words of appreciation. Use a large sheet of paper to provide enough space for the comments.

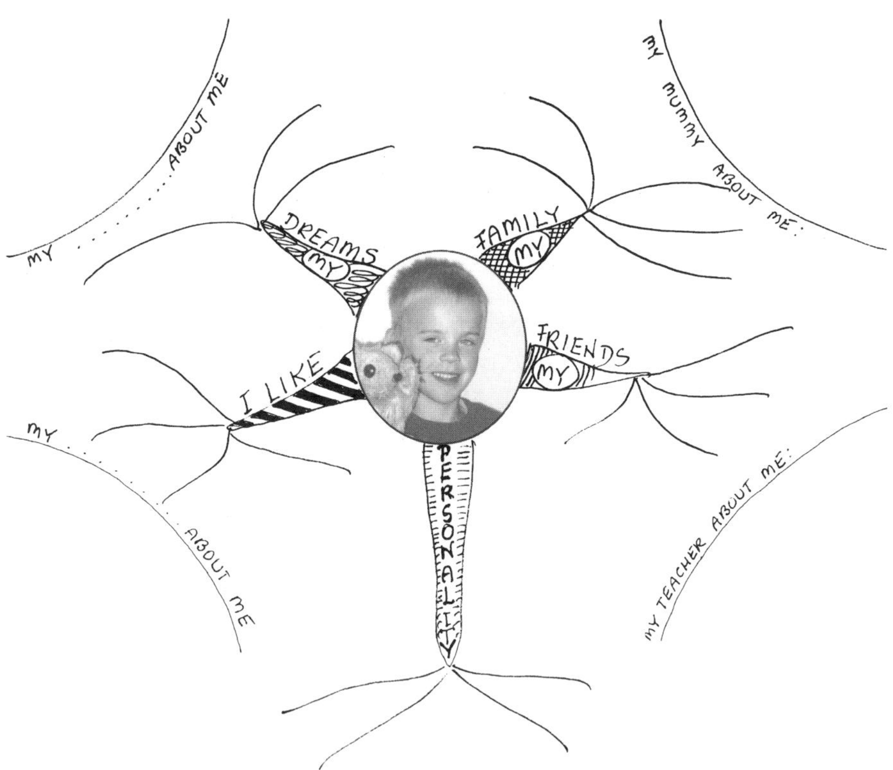

Every time your children look at the mind maps, they will feel empowered and truly proud of themselves.

Dear Parent,

Dear Teacher,

Dear Educator,

You have now done a tremendous amount of work with your child or children, as the case may be. You have acquired a great deal of experience and knowledge about learning, and about facilitating this fascinating process.

I am sure you have a lot of comments about the exercises, all of which are of great interest to me. I would be truly grateful if you could spare some time and share with me your observations, positive and negative comments about individual exercises, and anything you care to comment on.

With all my heart I wish you every success, a lot of joy and satisfaction. I also wish you a great deal of patience, strong determination, and openness to learning.

The best of luck to you and your children!

Please write to me at the address below:

Eva Hoffman,

Learn To Learn,

P.O. Box 29, Middlewich,

Cheshire CW10 9FN

references

[1] Hannaford, Carla. ***The Dominance Factor.*** Great Ocean Publications. Virginia (1997).

[2] White, Murray. ***Magic Circles: Building Self-Esteem Through Circle Time***. Lucky Duck Publishing. Bristol (1999).

[3] Branden, Nathaniel. ***Six Pillars of Self-Esteem***. Bantam Books. New York (1995).

[4] Stokes, Gordon and Whiteside, Daniel. ***One Brain: Dyslexic Learning Correction and Brain Integration***. Three In One Concepts. Burbank (1987).

[5] Dennison, Paul and Dennison, Gail. ***Brain Gym: Simple Activities For Whole Brain Learning***. Edu-Kinesthetics Inc. Glendale. California (1985).

[6] Palmer, Lyelle. ***Smooth Eye Pursuit Stimulation Readiness in Kindergarten, at Shingle Creek Elementary School.*** Minneapolis (1990-1991).

[7] Buzan, Tony. ***The Mind Map Book***. BBC Books. England (1993).

[8] Gardner, Howard. ***Frames Of Mind***. Basic Books. New York (1983).

recommended reading list

Here is a list of books you may find interesting and useful:

Beaver, Diana. ***Lazy Learning***. Element Books Ltd. England (1994).

Brewer, Chris and Campbell, Don G. ***Rhythms of Learning***. Zephyr Press. Arizona (1991).

Childre, Doc Lew. ***Teaching Children Love***. Planetary Publications. California (1996).

Dennison, Paul E. and Dennison, Gail E. ***Brain Gym (Teachers' Edition revised)*** Edu-Kinesthetics Inc. Ventura. California (1994).

De Porter, Bobbi. ***Quantum Learning***. Piatkus (1993).

Dryden, Gordon and Dr Vos, Jeannette. ***The Learning Revolution***. Accelerated Learning Systems. Unwin Brothers. England (1994).

Faber, Adele & Mazlish, Elaine. ***Liberated Parents, Liberated Children***. Avon Books. New York (1974).

Faber, Adele & Mazlish, Elaine. ***How To Talk So Kids Can Learn***. Fireside. Simon & Schuster. New York (1996).

Goelitz, Jeffrey. ***The Ultimate Kid***. University of the Trees Press. California (1986).

Hannaford, Carla. ***Smart Moves***. Great Ocean Publishers. Virginia (1995).

Kline, Peter. ***The Everyday Genius.*** Great Ocean Publishers. Virginia (1988).

McPhee, Dong. ***Limitless Learning.*** Zephyr Press. Arizona (1996).

Meister Vitale, Barbara. ***Unicorns Are Real***. Jalmar Press. California (1982).

Meister Vitale, Barbara. ***Free Flight - Celebrating Your Right Brain***. Jalmar Press. California (1986).

Mosley, Jenny. ***Circle Time***. Nasen Publication. England (1996).

Mosley, Jenny. ***More Quality Circle Time***. LDA. Cambridge (1998).

North, Vanda with Buzan, Tony. ***Get Ahead***. Buzan Centre Ltd. Dorset (1991).

O'Brien, Jonathan. ***Lightening Learning***. Quantum Training UK Ltd. (1998).

Olivier, Carolyn and Bowler, Rosemary F. ***Learning to Learn***. Simon and Schuster. New York (1996).

Rose, Colin. ***Accelerated Learning***. Topaz Publishing Limited. England (1985).

Rozman, Deborah. ***Meditating With Children***. Planetary Publications. California (1994).

Sims, Pamela. ***Awakening Brilliance***. Bayhampton Publications. Canada (1997).

White, Murray. ***Self Esteem. Its Meaning and Value at Schools***. Daniels Publishers. England (1996).